T0220231

Implementing iOS and macOS Documents with the Files App

Managing Files and Ensuring Compatibility

Jesse Feiler

Apress®

Implementing iOS and macOS Documents with the Files App: Managing Files and Ensuring Compatibility

Jesse Feiler
Plattsburgh, NY, USA

ISBN-13 (pbk): 978-1-4842-4491-3   ISBN-13 (electronic): 978-1-4842-4492-0
https://doi.org/10.1007/978-1-4842-4492-0

Managing Director, Apress Media LLC: Welmoed Spahr
Acquisitions Editor: Aaron Black
Development Editor: James Markham
Coordinating Editor: Jessica Vakili

Cover image designed by Freepik (www.freepik.com)

Distributed to the book trade worldwide by Springer Science+Business Media, New York, 233 Spring Street, 6th Floor, New York, NY 10013. Phone 1-800-SPRINGER, fax (201) 348-4505, e-mail orders-ny@springer-sbm.com, or visit www.springeronline.com. Apress Media, LLC is a California LLC and the sole member (owner) is Springer Science + Business Media Finance Inc (SSBM Finance Inc). SSBM Finance Inc is a **Delaware** corporation.

For information on translations, please e-mail rights@apress.com, or visit www.apress.com/rights-permissions.

Apress titles may be purchased in bulk for academic, corporate, or promotional use. eBook versions and licenses are also available for most titles. For more information, reference our Print and eBook Bulk Sales web page at www.apress.com/bulk-sales.

Any source code or other supplementary material referenced by the author in this book is available to readers on GitHub via the book's product page, located at www.apress.com/978-1-4842-4491-3. For more detailed information, please visit www.apress.com/source-code.

Printed on acid-free paper

Table of Contents

About the Author

Jesse Feiler is a developer, consultant, and author specializing in database technologies and location-based apps. Jesse's apps include NP Risk, Minutes Machine, Utility Smart, Cyber Continuity, and Saranac River Trail. He has worked for organizations as varied as the Federal Reserve Bank of New York (Chief, Special Projects Staff in Systems Development), the Albers and Archipenko foundations (data management), and a number of database projects typically using FileMaker. His apps are available in the App Store and are published by Champlain Arts Corp (`champlainarts.com`). Jesse is heard regularly on WAMC Public Radio for the Northeast's The Roundtable. He is a founder of Friends of Saranac River Trail, Inc. A native of Washington DC, he has lived in New York City and currently lives in Plattsburgh, NY.

About the Technical Reviewer

Charles Cruz is a mobile application developer for the iOS, Windows Phone, and Android platforms. He graduated from Stanford University with B.S. and M.S. degrees in engineering. He lives in Southern California and runs a photography business with his wife (www.bellalentestudios.com) and enjoys backpacking. Charles can be reached at codingandpicking@gmail.com.

CHAPTER 1

Using Documents

We use documents to store and organize data in the apps that we use.

This is a simple description of how and why we use documents with mobile apps built with macOS and iOS. There's much more than this simple description to consider when you start working with documents, and this chapter goes into the basic details you need to consider. You can find many books and articles dealing with documents, but the key points are described here.

Describing a Document

When you use an app, you sometimes need to store data for the app (that's the basic description just mentioned). Storing data turns out to be far from simple because when we talk about storing data, we almost always mean storing *and retrieving* data on demand. For that store-and-retrieve process to be useful to developers and users, you need to be able to *identify* the data to be stored and retrieved, such as the current temperature.

Just to make things a little more complex, you need to be able to store and retrieve data that you can identify in two different ways:

- You need to be able to identify the physical location of the data to be stored and retrieved.

- You need to be able to identify the logical characteristics of the data to be stored and retrieved.

© Jesse Feiler 2019
J. Feiler, *Implementing iOS and macOS Documents with the Files App*,
https://doi.org/10.1007/978-1-4842-4492-0_1

Putting this together means that you need to be able to store, retrieve, and identify data by its location and characteristics (such as a name).

Keeping Track of a Document and Its Data

We are accustomed to thinking of documents as static objects: once a document is written or printed, it doesn't appear to change. You can make changes or edits to documents, but those changes are typically visible in one way or another so that the initial document is modified. In the digital world, changes can be continual, and thinking of a document as a static object is misleading, to say the least.

When you use word processing tools, you can often track changes to documents so that instead of a static document you may have a multitude of changed documents. This multitude of changed documents can proliferate quickly not only with word processing documents but also with changes using tools such as Git or GitHub.

Structuring a Document

Documents can be structured in any way that the developer chooses. As you will see in Chapter 2, you can use structures that you create or common structures that are defined by others. The structure of a document provides a structure (or format) for the data that the document will contain. When you know a document's structure, you can read or write its data.

At least that is the idea. Document structures can change over time so in practice you need to know not only the structure of a document but the specific variation of the structure in use.

Note   The variation of a document's structure is often referred to as a *version*.

Handling Document Versions

A common way of handling the issue of document versions is to create a document structure that has at least two components: one is the version identifier and the second is everything else. For example, a document can start with the version identifier, which might be something as simple as a string or even an integer. In that way, your app will know to read a single integer or a string of X characters from the beginning of a document's data. That integer or string lets your app identify the version; having done that, your app can read the data for that version. This strategy is commonly used in macOS and iOS using a *file manager* (described in Chapter 2).

Comparing Documents and Files

Documents store data for an app in a known location from which it can be retrieved (or to which it can be stored). This location is typically a *file*—an object that is managed by the operating system. Like documents themselves, files can also have versions. A significant difference between a file and a document is that in many cases, the operating system manages a file's opening, closing, and storage. A document in many cases is inside a file.

Note   This is a simplification and generalization.

Structuring a Document and an App

Apps that are based on data are easy to build or convert to document-based apps. There are two common ways of building such apps. In the first way, developers start from a data structure and add functionality to it. In the other way, developers start from functionality and add data to it.

Summary

In this chapter, you saw an overview of documents, versions, and the differences between documents and files. From here you will move onto the details of documents and how to use them effectively.

Today, JSON (JavaScript Object Notation) and the `Codable` protocols are commonly used for managing app data. Previously, a technology referred to as *coding* was commonly used to store and manage data that is internal to an app. The basic process was to convert data that is identified by keys to and from `NSData` objects. The operating systems support `NSData`, and you don't have to worry about the implementation: it is fast and efficient. The only limitation is that not every type of data can be archived.

If you are building an app that needs to manage persistent data, chances are that Codable is the way to go. If you are modifying an existing app, you may want to continue using the archiving code that already exists. (Using both is perfectly feasibly, but it can become a maintenance nightmare.)

CHAPTER 2

Looking Inside a Document

In Chapter 1, you learned how to describe and structure a document. You now know that you, as the designer and developer of an app and its documents, control what data is stored, where and how it is stored, and how to identify and reference it.

You can decide that the data will be stored as a sequence of integers or as a single long string, whatever matters to you and the data you will use. In practice, it makes sense to structure the data inside a document if only to be able to access it easily. This chapter shows how to structure the data within a document using JSON encoding. This structure and encoding provides an easy-to-use format for data that relies on Unicode strings that can represent basic types recognized by JSON.

Using JSON Encoding

What matters most for JSON is the fact that the format is text-based (as opposed, for example, to a binary or digital representation) and the fact that each element can be named (as opposed to being identified by location or sequence).

© Jesse Feiler 2019
J. Feiler, *Implementing iOS and macOS Documents with the Files App*,
https://doi.org/10.1007/978-1-4842-4492-0_2

A location- or sequence-based coding style lets you specify the format of each element in the encoding sequence. Knowing the format of an element means that you know how much space it will take up, and this will let you read or write the data using the standard read/write syntax in any programming language.

The disadvantage of sequence- or location-based coding is that if you change the sequence of data elements or the format of a data element, you break any read/write code that you already have. JSON encoding relies on names of data elements rather than their formats or sequence. Thus, you avoid the frequent problem of breaking read/write code when you modify a format of a single data element or when you change the order of the data elements.

Introducing JSON

JSON starts as a text format for serialization of structured data. In this sense, *serialization* means converting the strings or other objects into a format that can be read or written. JSON starts from four primitive types, the meanings of which are common to many programming languages:

- A *string* is an ordered collection of Unicode characters.

- A *number* is just that; the most basic JSON number is a double.

- A *Boolean* is true or false.

- The final primitive value in JSON is *null*, an object that has no value.

In JSON, these types can be combined into *objects*, which are unordered collections of name/value pairs; a JSON *array* is an ordered collection of name/value pairs.

JSON and Swift

Swift goes beyond the basic JSON types with its `JSONSerialization` class (part of the Foundation framework). `JSONSerialization` converts JSON into array and dictionary Swift data types in addition to the basic JSON string, number, and Bool data types.

Note   Swift bridges Boolean and bool (C) types into Bool types. This is handled automatically for you.

Using Swift Structs

JSON is a flexible and easy-to-use notation tool. On the other hand, Swift is designed to be a powerful tool for building apps, particularly those using the model-view-controller (MVC) design pattern, which is more complex than JSON. One area that demonstrates this well is the Swift struct type. You may often declare structs in Swift that you will use throughout your app (or not at all). When you work strictly with JSON, it is uncommon to declare a struct that is not used to store data. This section explains how to create and use Swift structs with JSON.

Listing 2-1 shows how to create a Swift struct for a `Student` object or model (the terms are interchangeable in this section) using a playground.

Listing 2-1. Swift Struct

```
import Foundation

struct Student {
  var name: String
  var studentID: Int
}
```

What matters here is that the Student struct contains two var elements: name and studentID. Also worth noting is the fact that in this playground the Foundation framework must be imported because it will be used for working with JSON data. The other elements of the struct are standard Swift elements.

Tip   Note that the Swift style is to capitalize names of objects such as structs, so the name of the Student struct is capitalized.

With the struct shown in Listing 2-1, you can create an instance of the struct using code such as the following:

```
let student1 = Student(name: "John Appleseed", studentID: 154)
```

You can integrate JSON with Swift by using an encode (to: encoder) function to encode data along with an init (from decoder:) to do the reverse. To do this, you need to create keys to identify the elements that you will be coding and decoding. The first step is to declare coding keys as an enum CodingKeys element, as shown in Listing 2-2.

Listing 2-2. Swift Extension for Coding Keys

```
enum CodingKeys: String, CodingKey {
  case studentID = "studentID"
  case name
  }
}
```

Note that they are the keys you will use to encode and decode the data for the name and studentID variables. With the keys established along with the variables, you can now create an encode (to: encoder) function, as shown in Listing 2-3. Note that this extension indicates that the Student struct conforms to the Encodable protocol.

Listing 2-3. Swift Extension for Encoding

```
extension Student: Encodable {
  func encode(to encoder: Encoder) throws {
    var container = encoder.container(keyedBy: CodingKeys.self)
    try container.encode(name, forKey: .name)
    try container.encode(studentID, forKey: .studentID)
  }
}
```

Encoding JSON

You'll need a JSONEncoder object to handle encoding. Such a JSONEncoder object is often named jsonEncoder but you can use any name you want. A JSONEncoder object specifies the container for the encoded data.

In Listing 2-3, there is only one function, encode (to: encoder), and it uses a jsonEncoder object, the container that will contain the encoded data retrieved from the encoder.

The heart of the encode(to: encoder) function consists of the three lines of code that encode the struct elements (name and studentID).

The first of these lines tries to encode the name var using the .name key:

```
try container.encode(name, forKey: .name)
```

The second of these lines tries to encode the studentID var using the .studentID key:

```
try container.encode(studentID, forKey: .studentID)
```

These lines of code appear frequently in this type of function. In case you are wondering how the try is handled, note that the

```
func encode(to encoder: Encoder) function
```

can throw an error.

Tip   If you are debugging this code, set a breakpoint on the try statement so that you can see what causes a problem. Typical problems you may encounter in this code are typos in the key names.

Once you have created a jsonEncoder, you can reference the container within it and associate it with keys that you have declared elsewhere in the function with this line of code:

```
var container = encoder.container(keyedBy: CodingKeys.self)
```

Decoding JSON

Listing 2-4 shows the reverse operation to decode the JSON code.

Listing 2-4. Extension for Decoding

```
extension Student: Decodable {
  init(from decoder: Decoder) throws {
    let values = try decoder.container(keyedBy: CodingKeys.self)
    name = try values.decode(String.self, forKey: .name)
    studentID = try values.decode(Int.self, forKey: .studentID)
  }
}
```

Rather than an encode(to: encoder:) function, the heart of this code is init(from decoder: Decoder).

You retrieve the values from the decoder container using the coding keys, like so:

```
let values = try decoder.container(keyedBy: CodingKeys.self)
```

Rather than encode each variable and key, you then decode them using code such as the following:

```
name = try values.decode(String.self, forKey: .name)
studentID = try values.decode(Int.self, forKey: .studentID)
```

Putting the Encoding and Decoding Together

You can encode and decode the data as you wish. For the purpose of debugging, you can print out encoded data using code such as the following:

```
let student1 = Student(name: "John Appleseed", studentID: 154)          Student
let jsonEncoder = JSONEncoder()                                          Foundation.JSONEncoder
let jsonData = try jsonEncoder.encode(student1)                          41 bytes
print("encoded data:", jsonData)                                         "encoded data: 41 bytes\n"
```

You can print out a string showing the JSON code:

```
let jsonString = String(data: jsonData, encoding: .utf8)          "{"name":"John Appleseed","studentID":154}"
```

You can then reverse the process to print out the decoded data, as you see here:

```
let jsonDecoder = JSONDecoder()                                      Foundation.JSONDecoder
let student2 = try jsonDecoder.decode(Student.self, from: jsonData)  Student
print ("decoded data", student2)                                    "decoded data Student(name: "John Appleseed", studentID: 154)\n"
```

Note   For debugging, you may want to add the code in this section to your app so that you can use breakpoints to verify the encoding and decoding of the data. Usually once it is working and the keys are correct, you can disable the breakpoints or even remove them.

Summary

This chapter showed you how to encode and decode JSON data to and from Swift structs. Because you will be working with named Swift objects, you don't have to worry about the sequence or formatting of data.

CHAPTER 3

Matching a Document to a Document Format

In this chapter, you will see how to match a document as described and defined in your app's code to an actual runtime document object. This is the heart of putting documents to work. This chapter covers the three basic points you need to address:

- Preparing for iCloud

- Setting up your document in your app

- Managing document types

Preparing for iCloud

You may wonder what iCloud has to do with documents, but the answer is quite simple. As you start to use more and more aspects of iOS and macOS, you'll see that network connectivity and iCloud are no longer special cases. More and more you (and your users) will find that iCloud and the network are essential for your devices to function properly. It's taken a long time, but it's safe to say that we do have connectivity now.

Not only do we have connectivity most of the time, but users and developers are getting more comfortable with managing that connectivity. Developers and users alike turn to airplane mode when it's necessary to

© Jesse Feiler 2019
J. Feiler, *Implementing iOS and macOS Documents with the Files App*,
https://doi.org/10.1007/978-1-4842-4492-0_3

go offline for one reason or another. (This is a dramatic simplification from the days when it was common practice to separately adjust Bluetooth, data access, and other connections.)

Because iCloud connectivity is so common today, many developers include it in the capability settings for apps. Figure 3-1 shows the iCloud capability for a macOS app.

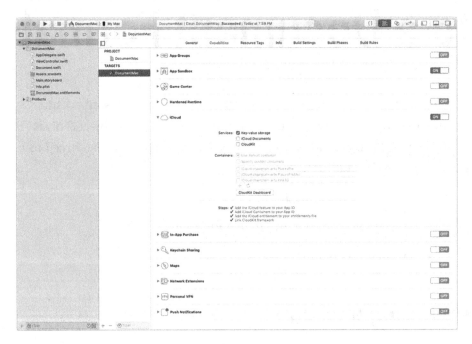

Figure 3-1. *Setting up iCloud for a macOS app*

The iCloud services can be turned on or off with the checkboxes. Note that iCloud documents can be enabled here. It's important to note as well that both CloudKit and key-value storage can be used with documents. You'll learn more about key-value storage with documents in Chapter 9.

For an iOS app, Figure 3-2 shows the cloud capability settings.

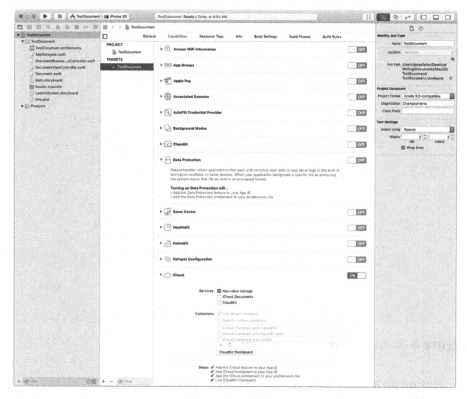

Figure 3-2. *Setting up iCloud for an iOS app*

Note that although there are many more options available for iOS apps, the section for the iCloud options is the same for iOS and macOS apps. For this reason, iCloud data is compatible with both environments.

Setting Up Your Document in Your App

There are differences in setting up and using documents in iOS and macOS; however, the basic settings, shown in Figures 3-3 and 3-4, are very similar. Figure 3-3 shows the document setup for an iOS app, and Figure 3-4 shows the setup for a macOS app.

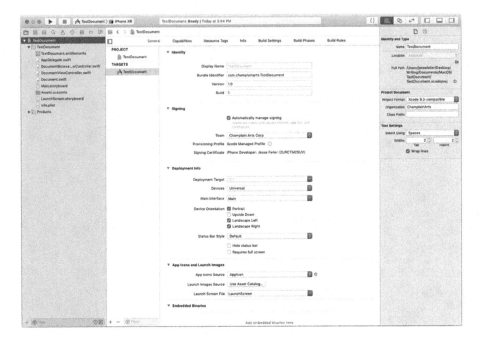

Figure 3-3. *Setting up a document in iOS*

Setting up a document in macOS is fairly similar, as you can see in Figure 3-4.

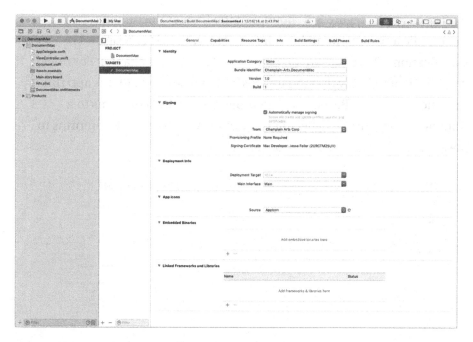

Figure 3-4. *Setting up a document in macOS*

Managing Document Types

An app can open many different documents depending on how you build the app and the documents. Each type of document (not each specific document) is defined as a document type in your info property list, as you can see in Figure 3-5.

Note that a document type has a name. In Figure 3-5, that name is Images; the document type name is descriptive and is used internally by your app.

A document type can handle various types of content. Apple uses uniform type identifiers (UTIs) to identify standard types. You can also create your own types. Using the standard types where possible makes your app more usable because users can read and write any files that conform to the supported UTIs.

For example, Figure 3-5 shows that the Images document type can handle any document that conforms to the `public.image` UTI specification. There is more on data types later in this chapter. For now, it is sufficient to know that the Images data type defined in this app (built with the Document Based App iOS project template) conforms to a standard image format called `public.image` which, in turn, conforms to the `public.data` and `public.content` UTIs.

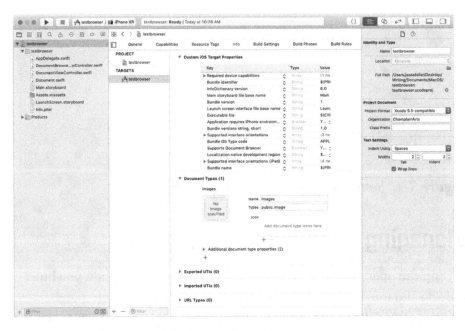

Figure 3-5. *The Images data type for iOS*

The simplest way to think about UTIs is

- **Document types** are the types of documents your app can open.

- **Exported UTIs** are the types of documents your app controls and can export (in a simple sense, they are the UTIs that your app writes).

- **Imported UTIs** are the types of documents your app
  reads. They are controlled by other apps, which export
  them.

Figure 3-5 shows a document type for an iOS app. There are different
settings for document types used in macOS. Some of the differences
revolve around the fact that in macOS, the document type is used to
determine what app opens that document type. In iOS, this is handled
differently.

Figure 3-6 shows a document type for macOS.

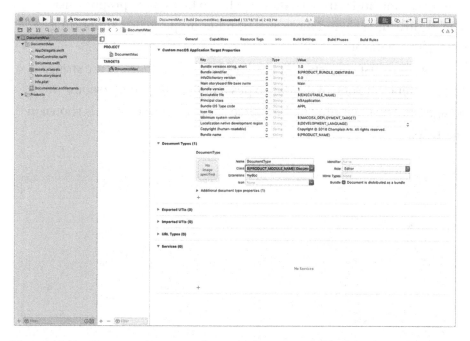

Figure 3-6. *Document types for macOS apps differ from iOS apps*

Looking at info.plist

What you see in Figures 3-5 and 3-6 is complex. In the project navigator
at the left of both figures, you see the project files. In both figures, you see
Swift files as well as one or more storyboards, entitlements files, and assets
(what you see varies by the project and your settings). What matters at
this point is the `info.plist` file, which is the property list for each project.
Property lists are used extensively in Cocoa and Cocoa Touch. They consist
of specific data types (arrays, strings, numbers, dictionaries, numbers,
dates, Boolean values, or NSData). Property lists are very fast and efficient
ways of storing and retrieving data. Each app has a basic property list
(called `info.plist`), and there may be other property lists supporting
other parts of the app.

A property list consists of key-value pairs where the keys are strings
and the values are one of the data types mentioned in the previous
paragraph. The beginning of the source code of a property list is shown in
Figure 3-7.

Figure 3-7. *Source code of a property list*

As you can see in Figure 3-7, a property list is easy to display in XML. The formatting that you see in Figure 3-7 is generated by Xcode. Property lists can also be formatted directly from XML in tools such as Excel and BBEdit. A property list displayed in Xcode can be formatted as shown in Figure 3-8.

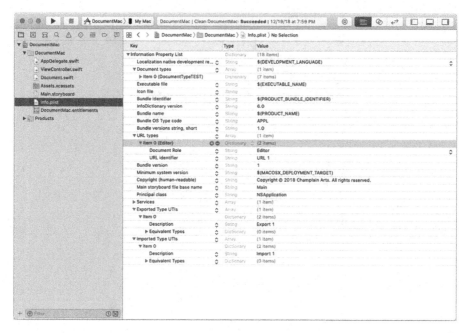

Figure 3-8. *Formatted property list in Xcode*

Note that with formatting, the property list is a bit easier to read, but remember that it is still the basic XML-based property list shown previously in Figure 3-7.

When you look at the project navigator, you can open any of the files using Control-click. For property lists, you are given a choice of the formatting options shown in Figure 3-9.

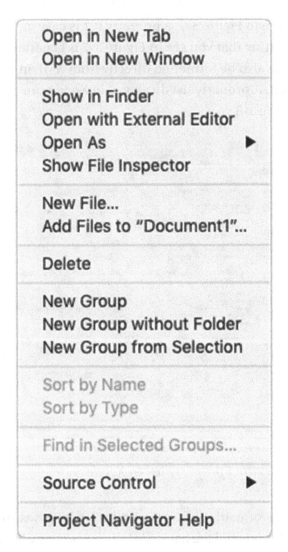

Figure 3-9. *Choosing a formatting option for a file in the Xcode project navigator*

Figure 3-10 shows the choices under the Open As option.

Figure 3-10. *Viewing a property list*

Source code formatting of a property list is shown in Figure 3-7; the property list format is shown in Figure 3-8.

If you refer back to Figures 3-5 and 3-6, you'll see in both of them a formatted property list at the top of the figure (remember that you can open it with a Control-click of the property list in the project navigator).

Beneath the formatted property lists in Figures 3-5 and 3-6 is yet another representation of the property list: it's simple to refer to it as a UI version. They are the versions shown for property types and other settings.

What matters is that all of the formatting you see in Figures 3-5 and 3-6 is based on the raw property list. The different UI formats can make it easier to work with the documents you want to handle in macOS or iOS. However, remember that the underlying property list (`info.plist`) is what matters. It is generally easier to work with the UI-formatted versions, but to be absolutely certain what you are doing, it is safest to go back to the source code of `info.plist` to see exactly what is going on.

Summary

Document types are used to match a document and its contents to a subclass of `UIDocument` or `NSDocument`. UTIs are used to identify documents that may be used by various apps and documents. In this chapter, you also explored the structuring and setting up of iCloud for documents and the use of property lists with files and documents.

CHAPTER 4

Securing and Protecting Data

As soon as you start thinking about saving data, you should be thinking about the security of that data. Every step of the process from deciding what data to store and what rules to implement for safeguarding that data needs to be considered. This chapter focuses on these issues.

Security and Privacy Overview

As pointed out at the beginning of Chapter 1, we use documents to store and organize the data that we use in apps. There are two fundamental types of data that we organize into documents: data that is distributed with the app, and data that users create and modify. The second type, which is data that users create and modify, may include data distributed with the app.

No matter what type of data is involved, if you are building or designing an app, you need to be aware of data issues that may arise. Until fairly recently, data issues were fairly modest in apps. Some data was clearly sensitive, but most data in apps required no special handling. Users and developers took frequent refuge behind the notion that "no one will care about our data." Data such as personal identification numbers was clearly sensitive; developers and users often handled security for such data by adding a disclaimer or note in the documentation.

© Jesse Feiler 2019
J. Feiler, *Implementing iOS and macOS Documents with the Files App*,
https://doi.org/10.1007/978-1-4842-4492-0_4

All of this started changing as massive data breaches were reported in a variety of systems. Best practices for the handling of sensitive data (or data that *might* be or become sensitive) were formulated.

In response to media reports and general awareness of data security, laws and regulations have begun to be implemented. For example, in the European Union (EU), the General Data Protection Regulation (GDPR) came into effect on May 25, 2018.

As new laws, regulations, and best practices take effect and become part of everyday operations, it behooves people who deal with data to understand how to implement these new practices in the modern data environment. This chapter provides a case study of a very simple use of private data and how it can be accidentally destroyed by simple or careless use. You can use this case study to guide you in your use of private data and privacy implementation.

Case Study: Using Cocoa Location Services

One of the most important privacy issues has to do with the location of mobile devices. Before mobile devices were so widespread, data privacy was mostly a matter of protecting information that was relatively static even if it was shared over the Internet. With mobile devices, however, the device itself can create confidential location data. This is a part of the necessary functioning of any device that needs to be able to locate itself and the infrastructure that it needs to use to make phone calls or otherwise do what it needs to do.

It is possible to disable some or all of the location services on a mobile device (for example, by using airplane mode) but this limits or degrades performance. Apple has made location services a feature that can be turned on and off directly rather than disabling all communications. To do so, you use the Cocoa Location Services Framework.

Users need to allow the use of location services on their device. Often this happens during installation of the operating system or setup of the device, but users can do it using Settings. Figure 4-1 shows how a user can set up the privacy location settings for an app using Settings.

Figure 4-1. *The Location Services settings*

Once you have located your app in the Location Services section, you can choose the privacy settings you want. An app can ask for your permission on an as-needed basis, as you can see in Figure 4-2. (The text at the top of the alert is explained later in this chapter.)

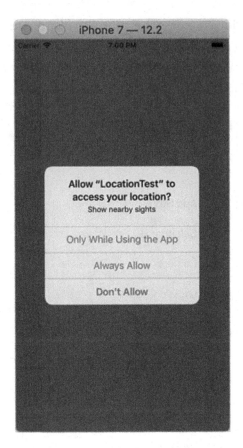

Figure 4-2. *Adjusting location privacy settings for an app as needed*

When using Settings, as shown in Figure 4-1, you can set the same options using the interface shown in Figure 4-3.

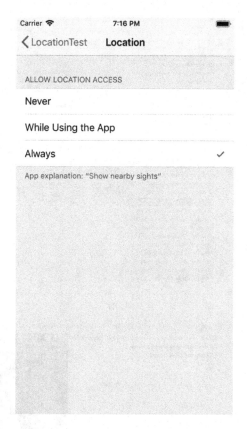

Figure 4-3. Using the same settings in the Settings app as in an alert from the app

In addition to the text in Settings and an app alert, you must adjust your property list to support these interfaces. As you can see in Figure 4-4, your property list has places where you describe how the user's location data will be used.

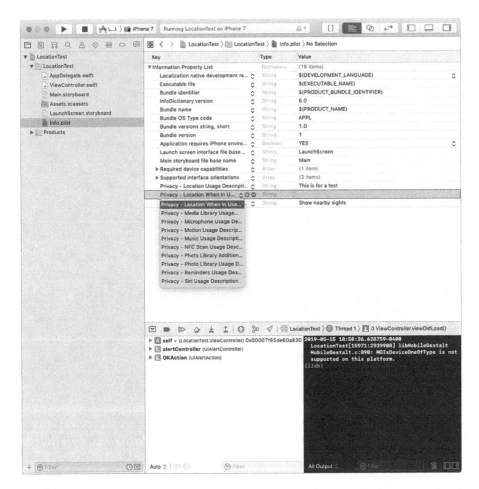

Figure 4-4. *Adjusting the property list for the privacy location settings*

It is very important to let the user know how you will use the location data you collect. Note that Apple reviewers ask developers to be specific in their description of how data will be used. It's no longer sufficient to explain your use of location data with a phrase such as "Get the user's location." Figure 4-5 shows an example of a description that is not specific enough.

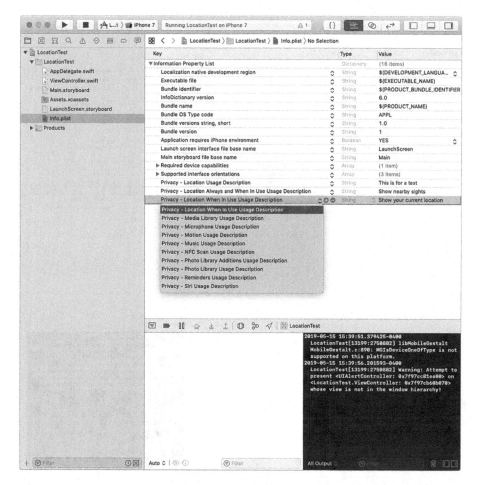

Figure 4-5. *Make sure you describe how you will use the data*

If you do not provide any description, your app will write a message to the console, as shown in Figure 4-6.

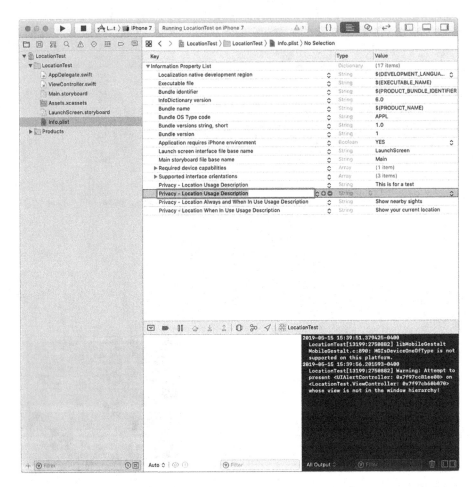

Figure 4-6. *A missing description prevents the app from getting the location*

Location services provide a great example of a common problem with privacy and security. If a description for the use of the location data is not provided, a runtime message is displayed in the console, but no error is thrown, as you can see in Figure 4-6. You can argue whether this should be an error or not (as the engineers at Apple most likely have done), but the argument is convincing that it is *not* an error even though it might be a programming mistake.

It is a common and usually good design to build this type of warning into an app. However, Figure 4-5 shows a common error. Note that the description is "This is a test." Because no error is thrown, it is remarkably easy for this description of how the location data will be used to show up in a shipping product. If you look at media reviews and articles about security, you'll see that one of the biggest complaints is that when an app does provide information about how data will be used, it may well be wrong. It is often a placeholder ("This is a test") or a description from another app that has been brought forward by copy-and-paste.

Summary

Because the explanations of what data is collected and how it will be used are written in simple language and not code that a compiler or build process can flag, these descriptions are very often wrong. Now that they are required by regulations such as GDPR, these errors are more important than ever.

The moral is that you should make certain that descriptions of security for users are correct so that users can rely on them, understand them, and use them.

CHAPTER 5

Implementing Documents on macOS: NSDocument

The heart of documents on macOS is the NSDocument class. Like UIDocument in iOS, it is an abstract class that you subclass for your own app. Three classes interact to provide document functionality in your app. They are the following:

- NSDocument is the abstract class that you subclass for your app.

- NSDocumentController is the app-specific class that manages the opening and closing of your document.

- NSWindowController is the class that manages the window in which your document is displayed.

© Jesse Feiler 2019
J. Feiler, *Implementing iOS and macOS Documents with the Files App*,
https://doi.org/10.1007/978-1-4842-4492-0_5

There isn't a one-to-one mapping of these classes between macOS and NSDocument and iOS and UIDocument; however, the similarities between NSDocument and UIDocument as well as the similarities between NSDocumentController and UIDocumentController are important (but they are no more than similarities).

Differences Between iOS UIDocuments and macOS NSDocuments

The biggest difference between iOS documents and macOS documents is that on macOS, the documents are part of the system environment and on iOS, they are part of each app's environment. There are reasons for this (many of which reflect the evolution of the two operating systems), but what matters is this aspect of the environment in which your app runs and your document exists.

Putting it another way, the tools that let you manage documents (creating and saving them, for example) are part of macOS and, on iOS they are part of tools such as UIDocumentBrowserViewController rather than iOS.

Creating a Document-Based App on macOS

As is usually the case, the simplest way to start building a new app is to use one of the built-in Xcode templates. Creating a document-based macOS app is no different. Start by creating a new project using the macOS Cocoa App template, shown in Figure 5-1.

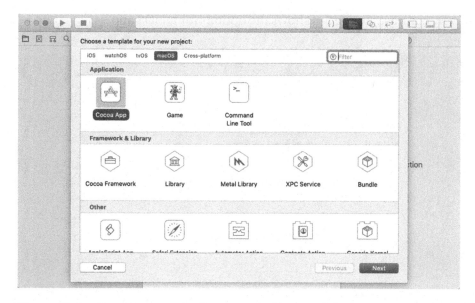

Figure 5-1. *Creating a new Cocoa app for macOS*

As you do with an iOS project, name the macOS project and provide optional information, as shown in Figure 5-2.

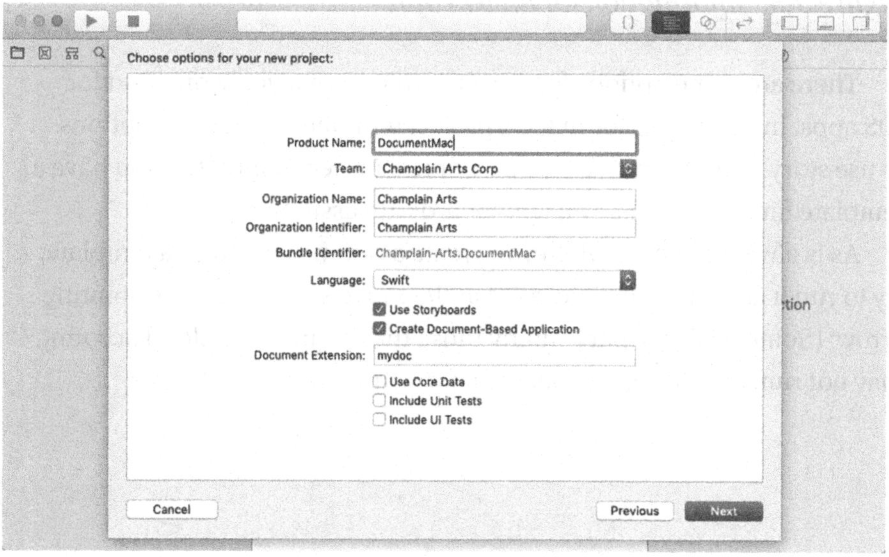

Figure 5-2. *Information for a macOS app*

By contrast, Figure 5-3 shows the options for an iOS app.

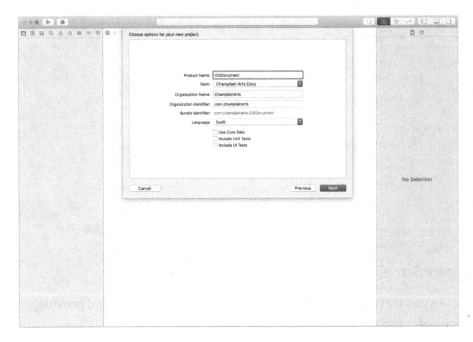

Figure 5-3. *Information for an iOS app*

There are some options for macOS projects that you won't find for iOS apps. In particular, for macOS project templates, you'll see options to use storyboards and documents. For iOS project templates, you have a template for documents, and storyboards are assumed.

As is always the case when you create a new project from a template, try to run it as you see in Figure 5-4 at the top left with the right-pointing arrow. (Some projects, particularly those that require an iCloud account, may not run, but this one should run for you.)

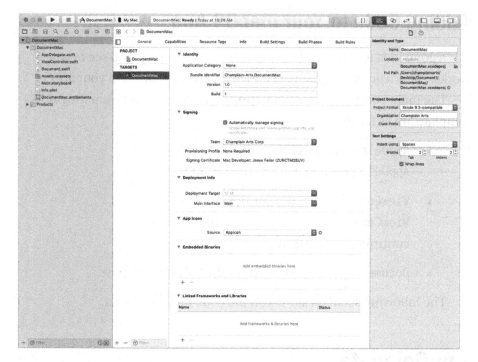

Figure 5-4. *Running the app*

As the project runs, it will use your Mac to run it instead of an iOS simulator. The basic app should show you a screen such as the one shown in Figure 5-5.

Figure 5-5. *Running your new macOS app*

Adding Code to Your macOS App

It is a good idea to look inside the app that you've created to see how it works. (This will help you make changes to it as you develop your app.)

The main components of your app when you start out from the project template are as follows:

- AppDelegate: This is functionally similar to the AppDelegate that you use for iOS apps.

- ViewController: This is a view controller (named ViewController) that works similarly to a view controller in an iOS app.

- Document: This is a subclass of the NSDocument class.

The following sections show you the code for this project.

AppDelegate

As you can see in Figure 5-6, this is similar to app delegates in iOS apps (but it's much shorter, in part because the operating system has much of the document work built into it).

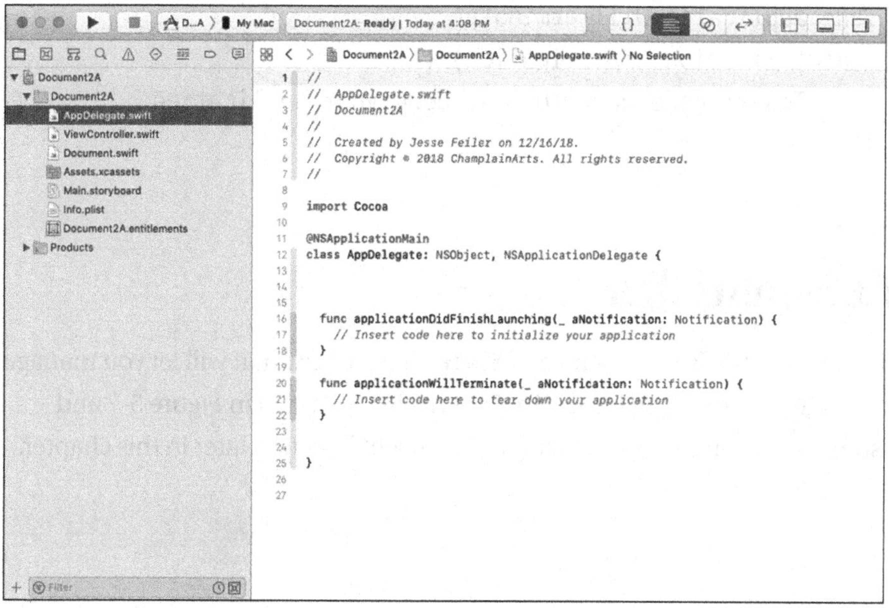

Figure 5-6. *Using AppDelegate*

The basic code that is part of the project template is shown in Listing 5-1. The comments in the code explain what you can add to it. The project template will run without any customization but you should implement the commented-out code or a variation of it before releasing an app even just for testing.

Listing 5-1. AppDelegate Template Code

```
import Cocoa

@NSApplicationMain

class AppDelegate: NSObject, NSApplicationDelegate {

  func applicationDidFinishLaunching(_
    aNotification: Notification) {
    // Insert code here to initialize your application
  }
```

```
func applicationWillTerminate(
  aNotification: Notification) {
  // Insert code here to tear down your application
}
}
```

ViewController

ViewController is the instance of NSViewController that will let you manage objects in the view. The basic ViewController is shown in Figure 5-7 and Listing 5-2. It will be modified in the "Document" section later in this chapter.

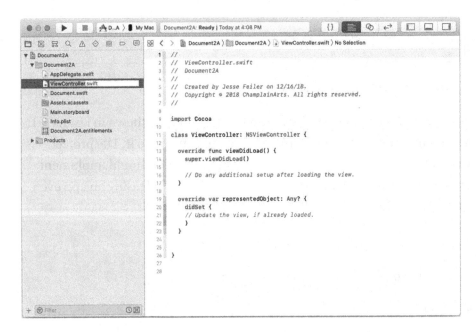

Figure 5-7. *Creating the ViewController*

Listing 5-2. ViewController Code

```
//
//  ViewController.swift
//  Document2A
//
//

import Cocoa

class ViewController: NSViewController {

  override func viewDidLoad() {
    super.viewDidLoad()

    // Do any additional setup after loading the view.
  }

  override var representedObject: Any? {
    didSet {
    // Update the view, if already loaded.
    }
  }
}
```

Document

Document is the subclass of NSDocument that manages the document and its data. The basic code is shown in Figure 5-8 and Listing 5-3. It is important to note that the document subclass makeWindowControllers method includes the code for matching the storyboard to the Document class.

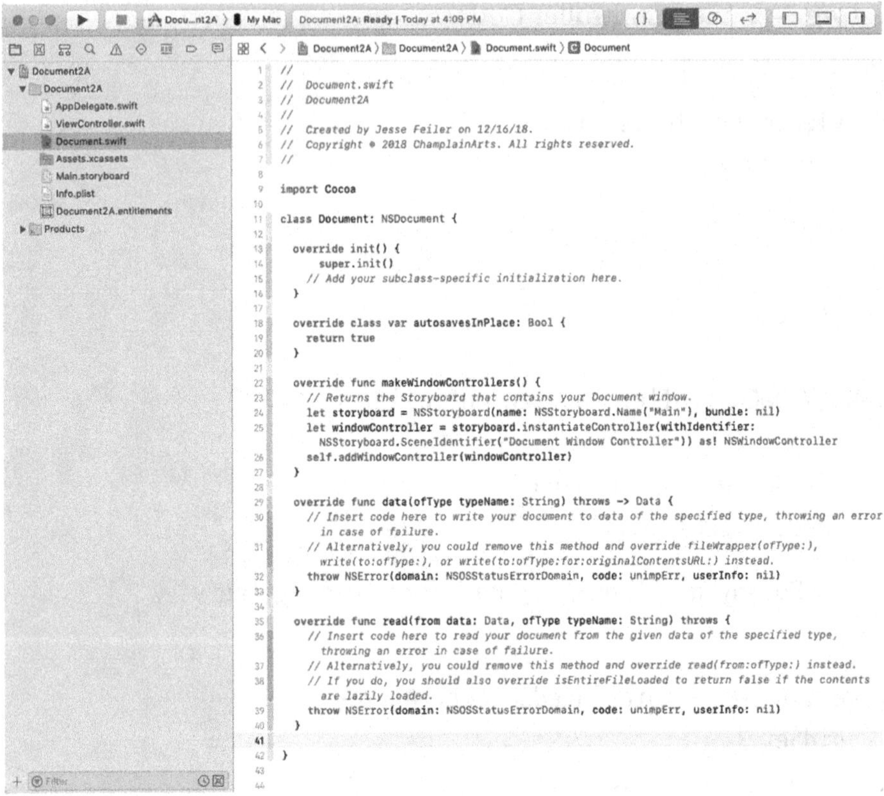

Figure 5-8. *Managing your document*

Listing 5-3. Document Code

```
//
//  Document.swift
//  Document2A
//
//

import Cocoa

class Document: NSDocument {
```

```swift
override init() {
  super.init()

  // Add your subclass-specific initialization here.
}

override class var autosavesInPlace: Bool {
  return true
}

override func makeWindowControllers() {
  // Returns the Storyboard that contains your
    Document window.
  let storyboard = NSStoryboard(
    name: NSStoryboard.Name("Main"), bundle: nil)
  let windowController =
    storyboard.instantiateController(
      withIdentifier:
        NSStoryboard.SceneIdentifier(
          "Document Window Controller"))
      as! NSWindowController
  self.addWindowController(windowController)
}

override func data(ofType typeName: String) throws -> Data {
  // Insert code here to write your document to data of the
  // specified type, throwing an error in case of failure.
  // Alternatively, you could remove this method and override
  // fileWrapper(ofType:), write(to:ofType:), or
  // write(to:ofType:for:originalContentsURL:) instead.

  throw NSError(domain: NSOSStatusErrorDomain
    code: unimpErr, userInfo: nil)
}
```

```
override func read(from data: Data,
  ofType typeName: String) throws
  {
  // Insert code here to read your document from the
  // given data of
  // the specified type, throwing an error in case of failure.
  // Alternatively, you could remove this method and override
  // read(from:ofType:) instead.
  // If you do, you should also override isEntireFileLoaded to
  // return false if the contents are lazily loaded.

  throw NSError(domain: NSOSStatusErrorDomain,
    code: unimpErr, userInfo: nil)
  }
}
```

Storyboard

Figure 5-9 shows how you can modify the storyboard in the template to add a text view (you do this just as you do it in iOS). In Document, you can use the text view to collect the data and then process it.

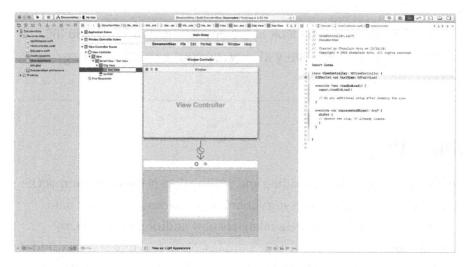

Figure 5-9.

Overview of macOS and iOS Development

Note that the details of managing the data in the text views differ between macOS and iOS. Among the differences are that in macOS, functions expose scrolling behaviors that in iOS are properties of the views.

Keep in mind the history of Cocoa on macOS. In the earliest documentation, OpenStep and its precursor, NeXTSTEP, were designed for use in a world of business apps that were running on early personal computers. Even the earliest versions had functions for managing formatted tables and strings. The development path for Cocoa and Cocoa Touch differs in large part because the target platform for Cocoa Touch was at first the iPhone. Although there were (and are) business apps, the apps and users of iOS devices are very different from the apps and users of NeXTSTEP at its launch (September 18, 1989).

> **Note**   For an interesting look at the environment in 1989, see the Timeline of Computer History at `www.computerhistory.org/timeline/1989/`.

Summary

The basic mechanism for reading and writing data is the same for macOS and iOS: you use objects in a storyboard to receive and send that data.

Note that storyboards are a relatively new addition to macOS, so you may not find them in old code samples. Note, too, that you may find references to binding in old code. Although it is not deprecated, it is not used frequently in modern macOS code.

CHAPTER 6

Implementing Documents on iOS

There are three main issues you have to consider when implementing documents on iOS:

- With the advent of the iOS Files app in iOS 11, users began to have access to the underlying file system in iOS.

- The basic class for iOS documents is `UIDocument`, which is designed to be subclassed.

- `UIDocumentBrowserViewController` is a view controller designed to implement the user interface of the Files iOS app.

This chapter focuses on the first point: Files.

Using Files and the iOS File System

When the first iPhone was launched, it wasn't an immediate success. In fact, if you go back and search for news articles, you'll discover some major complaints about the product. One of the biggest was the absence of connectors (such as USB) to attach other devices to the iPhone in the way that users were accustomed to attaching devices to personal computers.

© Jesse Feiler 2019
J. Feiler, *Implementing iOS and macOS Documents with the Files App*,
https://doi.org/10.1007/978-1-4842-4492-0_6

The fact that the entire iPhone file system was hidden from the user's view was one of the common complaints. There were reasons for the hidden file system architecture and, over the decade of iPhone use, users, developers, and analysts have come to learn the benefits (and sometimes, drawbacks) of this architecture.

With the advent of iOS 11 in 2017, Apple released its Files app, which approached the issue of file management in a very different way from the architecture that people were accustomed to from the beginning of the personal computer era. In the basic personal computer file architecture, which was built on the traditional Unix file architecture, users managed files and folders, which could be placed almost anywhere on the device. The Files app takes a different approach in that files are accessible from specific areas that are usually related to apps. In other words, instead of thinking of files that can be moved anywhere on a personal computer's disk, users are now encourage to think of files that can be moved anywhere within an app's file space (often referred to as a *sandbox*).

Recognizing that people are not simply using disk space on a personal computer, the Files app incorporates access to cloud storage services that go beyond a personal computer such as iCloud, Dropbox, Box, Google Drive, and OneDrive.

For people who are accustomed to the legacy structure where users can place files where they want to, this can be a relearning experience. Perhaps the most important point to consider is that with the legacy file structure, you place files where you want to place them in relation to your computer's disks and other storage locations. Using the iOS File System and Files, you place files in either of two general locations:

- You can place files in the folder for a specific app. A folder can be shared among several related apps. For good examples of this type of sharing, use the built-in Pages, Keynote, or Numbers apps and experiment by saving files to be shared.

- You can place files in a cloud storage service such as iCloud or Dropbox.

Here are some details about using Files.

Choosing Document Storage Locations

Remember that file storage is primarily determined by the app a file is associated with. Your primary tool for choosing the storage location is by setting it in Settings for an app. For example, in Settings, you can see the various settings for installed apps on your iOS device (Figure 6-1).

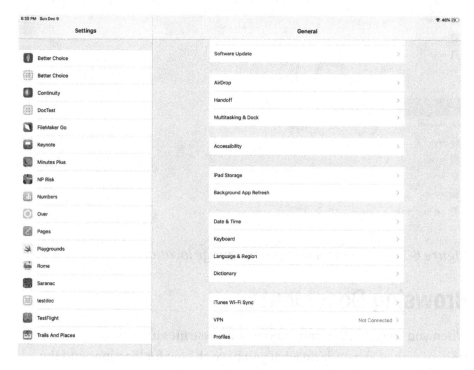

Figure 6-1. *Choosing the settings for your apps*

Find your app and then choose the storage location, as shown in Figure 6-2. Your choices depend on what you have installed on your iOS device. If you use iCloud (a very common choice), you can choose to store your data there. You can choose to store it on a local device or you can use Dropbox, Box, or another service.

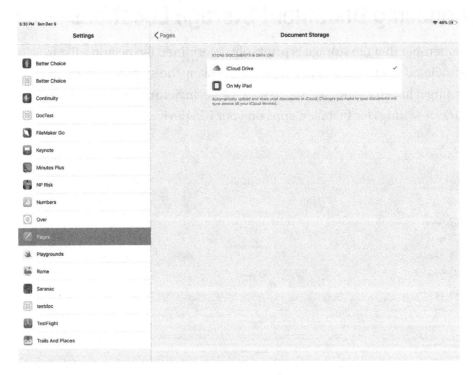

Figure 6-2. *Choosing a document storage location*

Browsing Documents

When you use Files, you can choose to browse files in a specific location (this, of course, depends on what you have chosen for locations and the files that you have). It's important to understand the browsing data that Files shows you, so the following images show you what you might see.

If you have decided to use your iPad for storage, you might see the
browse results shown in Figure 6-3 when you choose the On My iPad
location.

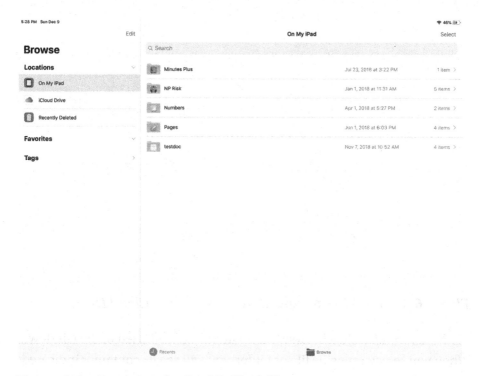

Figure 6-3. *Browsing the On My iPad files*

If you use iCloud Drive, you may see a browse window such as the one
shown in Figure 6-4.

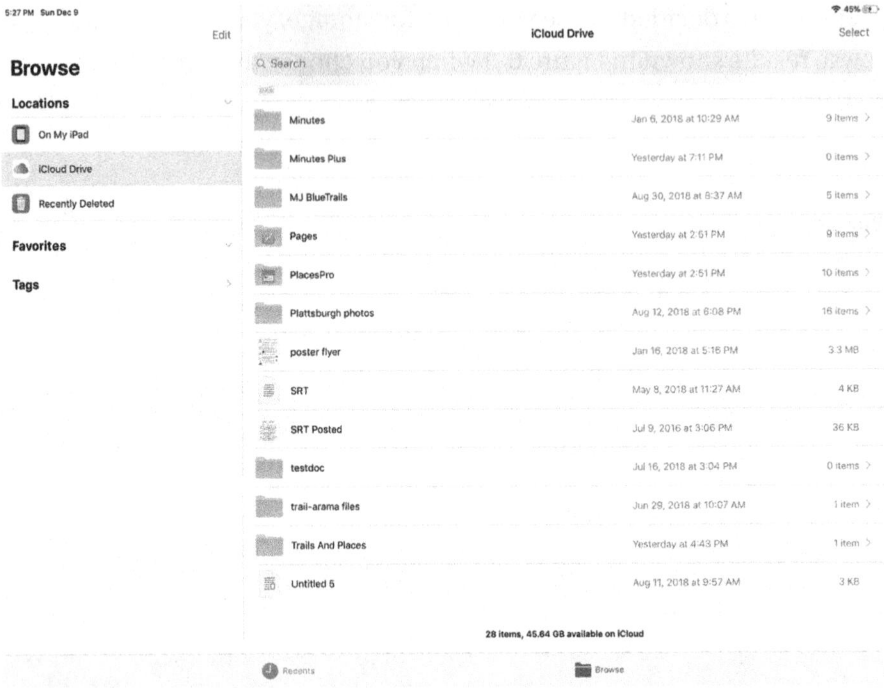

Figure 6-4. *Browsing documents and folders on iCloud Drive*

Note that when you browse, the locations are at the left of the window. When you select a specific file or folder, you will see its container indicated either in Locations at the left or at the top of the right-hand list, as in Figure 6-5.

Figure 6-5. *Folder names at the top of the right-hand pane*

Looking at Recent Documents

Using the tabs at the bottom of the window, you can switch between recent files and folders and ones that you want to browse. Figure 6-6 shows recent files and folders.

Figure 6-6. *Recent files and folders*

If some of your documents have not yet been downloaded from a remote server, you will see the cloud icon shown in Figure 6-7, indicating that they are waiting to be downloaded. If you tap a specific file, you can speed up its downloading process.

Figure 6-7. *Downloading files*

Note that in addition to indicating if a file needs to be downloaded, you can see its location. For example, in Figure 6-7, in the lower right, you can see a document that is marked as On My iPad rather than iCloud Drive.

Tip   Get used to working with Files and using the file location information and download status. Because there is often a time lag as a download is scheduled and processed, you will save yourself time if you know what files are where so that you don't try to debug issues that are merely timing issues.

Viewing Files and Folders for an App

When you look at apps on an iOS device, you can tap and hold an app icon to see the files and folders that may belong to it, as shown in Figure 6-8.

Figure 6-8. *Tap and hold an app icon to see its files*

If necessary, a Show More button will appear at the top right, as you can see in Figure 6-8. When you use Show More, a companion Show Less button appears, as you can see in Figure 6-9.

Figure 6-9. *The Show Less option*

When you look at the apps in Files (Figure 6-7), you will see a list of the files and folders, as shown in Figure 6-10.

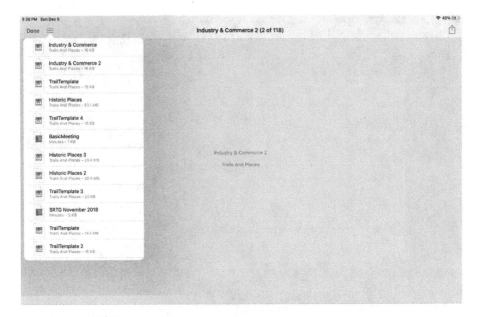

Figure 6-10. *A list of all files and folders for an app*

Summary

Use Settings to control where you store the files and folders for an app, and use Files to browse files and folders as well as recents.

Remember that you control where the files and folders are placed not by selecting locations on your personal computer but by selecting locations on the device you're using or on a cloud storage function such as iCloud or Dropbox.

CHAPTER 7

Implementing Documents on iOS: UIDocument and UIDocumentBrowser ViewController

Documents are critical components of many apps and have been so from the beginning of the personal computer era. Many people still think of documents as paper-based objects, but the documents that people work with today on iOS and macOS are much more sophisticated than their paper predecessors. This chapter introduces today's documents and their structures. It then explains how to use `UIDocumentBrowserViewController` to manage documents.

© Jesse Feiler 2019
J. Feiler, *Implementing iOS and macOS Documents with the Files App*,
https://doi.org/10.1007/978-1-4842-4492-0_7

Creating a Document-Based App

As is often the case with the basic building blocks of the frameworks in
Xcode, the simplest way to get started with documents for iOS is to use the
Document Based App project template that's built into Xcode. Begin by
creating a new iOS project, as shown in Figure 7-1.

Figure 7-1. *Picking the Document Based App template in Xcode*

Go through the standard options shown in Figure 7-2 to set up the
template.

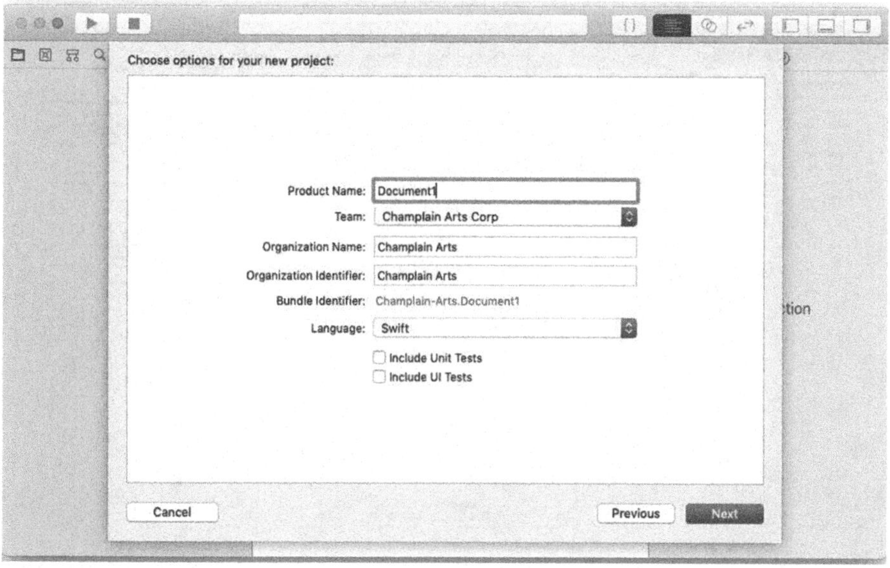

Figure 7-2. *Setting the options for the new project*

Continue with the options until you have the project template complete as shown in Figure 7-3.

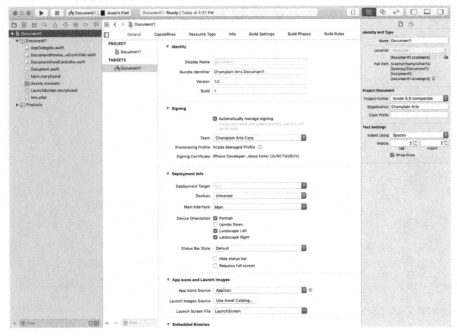

Figure 7-3. *Reviewing the new project*

When you're finished, run the app. (This is a step you should always take when you create a new project from a template. Except for issues such as network availability, your new project template should run.)

As you can see in Figure 7-4, you can open the project and see the
storyboard with two view controllers.

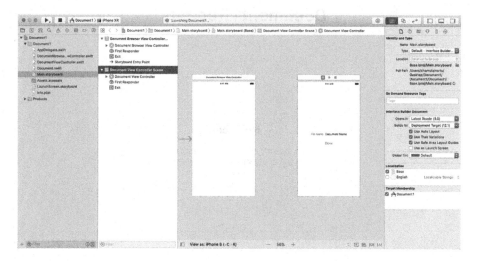

Figure 7-4. *Looking at the storyboard*

Run the project. You should see the Simulator, as shown in Figure 7-5.

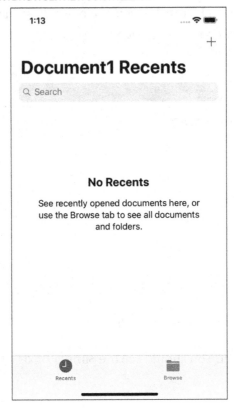

Figure 7-5. *Running the app*

Continue exploring your new app. Use the Browse tab to browse files in your app's sandbox, as shown in Figure 7-6.

Figure 7-6. *Exploring the Browse tab in your app*

There are no files there now, but there is a Create Document button.
Try it out!

Nothing happens.

It's time to move to the next section of this chapter, which looks at
UIDocument. Among other tasks, you'll see how to implement the Create
Document button.

Introducing UIDocument

The basic document class in iOS is UIDocument. UIDocument provides the basic functionality of a document in these ways:

- **fileURL**: UIDocument identifies a document using a file URL so that your app can locate it for reading and writing.

- UIDocument manages **asynchronous reading and writing** of data on a background queue with minimal effort on your part.

- UIDocument also coordinates reading and writing of document files using **cloud services** such as iCloud.

- UIDocument also manages **conflicts and changes to versions** of your document.

These are the basic components of UIDocument. In order to start working with documents, you can use the basic code that is available in the Document Based App template. The basic code in the project template provides functionality for fileURL (document identification) as well as the critical reading and writing features along with cloud services and management of conflicts and changes.

Working with UIDocument

The key components for working with UIDocument are UIDocument, which handles reading, writing, and creating UIDocuments, and UIDocumentBrowserViewController, which handles the browsing and the user interface part of reading, writing, and creating UIDocument. Completing the basic functionality of UIDocument is an implementation of UIDocumentViewController.

UIDocument takes care of a lot of document management for you
including many critical functions such as saving documents and managing
changes. You can study the documentation to see all of the features, but
you can use the stripped-down functions for UIDocument that are part
of the Document Based App template used in this chapter. In fact, the
basic code from the template (shown in Figure 7-7 and Listing 7-1) is an
excellent place to start and, for many basic apps, it may be all you need
along with a line or two of app-specific code.

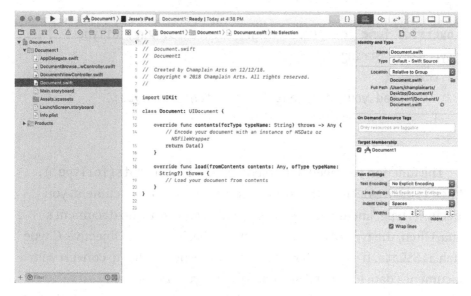

Figure 7-7. *Basic UIDocument functionality*

Listing 7-1. The Basic Code

```
//
//  Document.swift
//  Document1
//
//
```

```swift
import UIKit

class Document: UIDocument {

  override func contents(forType typeName: String) throws ->
  Any {
    // Encode your document with an instance of NSData or
       NSFileWrapper
    return Data()
  }

  override func load(fromContents contents: Any, ofType
  typeName: String?)
    throws {
      // Load your document from contents: ofType:)
    }
}
```

The function you need to implement first is `contents(forType:)`.
When you have decided the format for the data in your document, you
specify its type, and that type is used to read and write the document's
data. Often, the type of a document file is a basic Swift or Objective-C type
such as NSData. If you use NSData, it is your responsibility to convert your
document's data to NSData or whatever type you are using.

The companion function is `load(fromContents: ofType:)`. Both of
these functions let you read or write a general-purpose format and then
convert it into data that your app manages.

If you explore the code for UIDocument, you'll see that it handles
asynchronous reading and writing, working with cloud data, and
managing changes all within the basic structure of the two functions:
`contents(forType:)` and `load(fromContents: ofType:)`

Working with UIDocumentViewController

Once you have your document in place, you need to add a view controller so that you can see and manipulate content. In the Document Based App project template, the document controller is created as shown in Figure 7-8.

Figure 7-8. *The DocumentViewController*

The code is shown in Listing 7-2.

Listing 7-2. Document View Controller Code

```swift
class DocumentViewController: UIViewController {

  @IBOutlet weak var documentNameLabel: UILabel!

  var document: UIDocument?

  override func viewWillAppear(_ animated: Bool) {
    super.viewWillAppear(animated)
```

71

```
  // Access the document
  document?.open(completionHandler: { (success) in
  if success {
    // Display the content of the document, e.g.:
    self.documentNameLabel.text
        self.document?.fileURL.lastPathComponent
      } else {
        // Make sure to handle the failed import
        appropriately,
        // e.g., by presenting an error message to the user.
      }
    })
  }

@IBAction func dismissDocumentViewController() {
  dismiss(animated: true) {
    self.document?.close(completionHandler: nil)
  }
 }
}
```

There are two functions in the DocumentViewController class:
viewWillAppear((_:) and dismissDocumentViewController(). The
first opens the document and the second closes it.

Opening the Document

Opening the document is a great example of the Swift asynchronous
programming style using a completion handler. The code is

```
document?.open(completionHandler: { (success) in
  if success {
```

```
// Display the content of the document, e.g.:
self.documentNameLabel.text
self.document?.fileURL.lastPathComponent
} else {
    // Make sure to handle the failed import appropriately,
    // e.g., by presenting an error message to the user.
    }
})
```

open is called on the document (note that it is an optional and is unwrapped
with ?). The completion handler is declared in the open function, and it
is called upon completion of open. There is one parameter passed into
the completion handler. As is common but not required, it is often called
success; it is a Boolean that indicates if open has succeeded or not.

The completion handler then executes this code:

```
if success {
    // Display the content of the document, e.g.:
    self.documentNameLabel.text
    self.document?.fileURL.lastPathComponent
} else {
    // Make sure to handle the failed import appropriately, e.g., by
    // presenting an error message to the user.
}
```

For a successful opening of the document, a label in the storyboard is
filled with lastPathComponent of the file URL. (You can see this at the right
in Figure 7-4.) For most apps, you would actually display some content
from the document in the interface.

Note   The completion handler for opening the document is a
significant way of improving app performance. When you are dealing
with documents and files that may be in the cloud, the delay in
executing the completion handler (whether successful or not) can be
significant. Remember this when you are testing your app.

Closing the Document

Closing the document uses a similar structure with
dismissDocumentViewController. However, note that the completion
handler in the app is nil. If you don't need to process data that has
changed, you don't have to do anything except close the document.

Working with UIDocumentBrowserView Controller

UIDocumentBrowserViewController is the heart of the document-based
app. This section provides an overview of what happens. There are
two basic paths to follow: creating a document or opening an existing
document. (You might want to refer back to Figures 7-5 and 7-6.)

Loading the UIDocumentBrowserViewController

The first step in working with a UIDocumentBrowserViewController is to
load it, as shown in Figure 7-9.

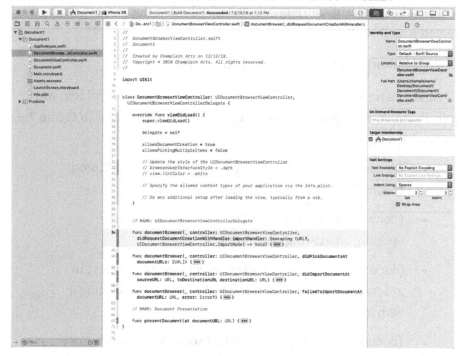

Figure 7-9. *Loading UIDocumentBrowserViewController*

Note that your UIDocumentBrowserViewController subclass should
also conform to the UIDocumentBrowserViewControllerDelegate
protocol. You can see this in line 12 of Figure 7-9. For additional reference,
here is the code:

delegate = self

You have choices for the visual style of the browser that you can
set at this point so that they coordinate with your user interface. Other
initializations can be handled in your info.plist.

Note   There is more on your info.plist in Chapter 3.

75

Note that `viewDidLoad` lets you choose whether documents can be created with line 19:

```
allowsDocumentCreation = // true or false
```

After you have loaded the `UIDocumentBrowserViewController`, you typically implement four functions, which are shown as stubs in Figure 7-9, The functions are

- `(documentBrowser(_:didRequestDocumentCreationWithHandler:)` for creating a new document

- `(documentBrowser(_:didPickDocumentAt:)` for opening an existing document

- `(documentBrowser(_:didImportDocumentAt:toDestinationURL:)` for, after opening a document, presenting it with its content

- `(documentBrowser(_:failedToImportDocumentAt:error)` to handle an error

Creating a Document

You can use the template to create a new document. As the documentation indicates, you can allow users to choose which of several basic documents you will use as a template. See Figure 7-10.

Figure 7-10.   *Creating a document*

In many older design patterns, you would choose to create an empty
document and then possibly modify it with data. The design pattern that
is most often used in iOS is not to create a document but instead to copy
an existing template document from your bundle and put the copy in the
appropriate place for your app. This is a different work flow, but it becomes
more efficient as you create and modify your app over time.

Listing 7-3 shows the code to let users choose a template from a list.
The key line of code is

```
let newDocumentURL = Bundle.main.url(forResource: "Template",
  withExtension: DocumentBrowserViewController.
  documentExtension)
    importHandler(newDocumentURL, .copy)
}
```

This takes a file called Template with your document extension from
your bundle and copies it to a new location. If you don't need to let users

choose from among several templates, just use this code without the alert
that lets people choose.

Listing 7-3. Letting Users Choose a Template

```
let title = NSLocalizedString("Choose File Template", comment: "")
let cancelButtonTitle = NSLocalizedString("Cancel", comment: "")
let defaultButtonTitle = NSLocalizedString("Basic (Default) ",
  comment: "Default")
let generalButtonTitle = NSLocalizedString("Demo)", comment: "")
let alertController = UIAlertController(title: title, message:
message, preferredStyle: .alert)

let newDocumentURL = Bundle.main.url(forResource: "Template",
  withExtension: DocumentBrowserViewController.
  documentExtension)
    importHandler(newDocumentURL, .copy)
  }

// Create the actions.
let cancelAction = UIAlertAction(title: cancelButtonTitle,
  style: .cancel) { action in
    importHandler(nil, .none)
  }

let defaultButtonAction = UIAlertAction(title:
defaultButtonTitle,
  style: .default) { _ in
    let newDocumentURL = Bundle.main.url(forResource: "Template",
      withExtension: DocumentBrowserViewController.
      documentExtension)
        importHandler(newDocumentURL, .copy)
      }
```

```
let generalButtonAction = UIAlertAction(title:
generalButtonTitle,
  style: .default) { _ in
    let newDocumentURL = Bundle.main.url(forResource:
    "Template2",
      withExtension: DocumentBrowserViewController.
      documentExtension)
        importHandler(newDocumentURL, .copy)

}

// Add the actions.
alertController.addAction(cancelAction)
alertController.addAction(defaultButtonAction)
alertController.addAction(generalButtonAction)

present(alertController, animated: true, completion: nil)
```

Picking (Opening) a Document

Figure 7-11 shows the code for opening an existing document.

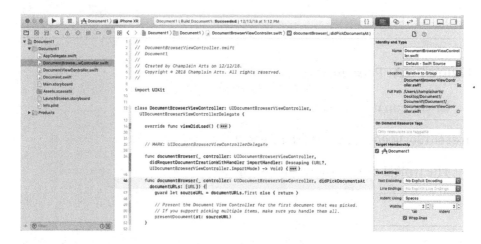

Figure 7-11. *Opening an existing document*

The key line of code here lets you select from several existing files; you
attempt to open the first in the list as specified here:

```
guard let sourceURL = documentURLs.first else { return }
```

As you can see in Figure 7-9, you can specify if multiple
files can be selected with this line of code in viewDidLoad for
DocumentBrowserViewController:

```
allowsPicking Multiple Items = // true or false
```

Once you have picked a document, you ask the
DocumentBrowserViewController to present it, as shown in Figure 7-12.

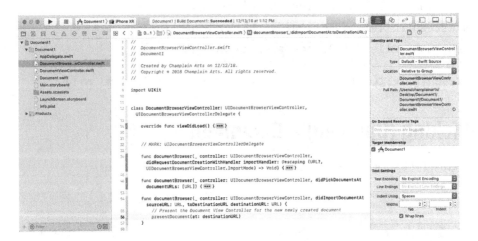

Figure 7-12. *Presenting a document*

Or you can use this code:

```
presentDocument (at:destinationURL)
```

The typical code is shown in Listing 7-4.

Listing 7-4. Presenting a Document

```
func presentDocument(at documentURL: URL) {

  let storyBoard = UIStoryboard(name: "Main", bundle: nil)
  let documentViewController =
    storyBoard.instantiateViewController(withIdentifier:
    "DocumentViewController") as! DocumentViewController
  documentViewController.document =
    Document(fileURL: documentURL)

  present(documentViewController, animated: true,
    completion: nil)
}
```

Note that this code brings together a document view controller, a
storyboard, and a document. All of these components must match (this is
a common cause of debugging issues).

The code is also shown in Figure 7-13.

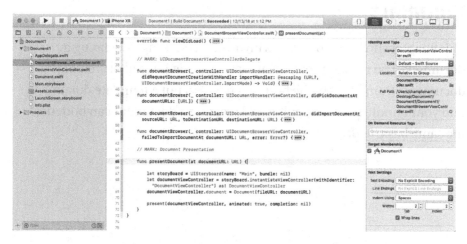

Figure 7-13. *Presenting a document*

Handling Errors

The last part of handling document browser view controllers is to make
certain that you handle errors properly; see Figure 7-14.

Figure 7-14.   Handling errors properly

Summary

This chapter shows the processes involved in opening or creating a
document. The most important take-away is that instead of creating
documents from scratch, the best practice is to put a template document
into your bundle so that opening and creating a document can both use
the same basic code.

CHAPTER 8

Sharing Documents with Share Buttons

In previous chapters, you saw how to implement documents on iOS and macOS to save data and share it across your apps. In this chapter, you'll see another way to share data using the Share button so that you can dynamically share data from one app to another without using a document to store and share the data.

The main points covered in this chapter are

- Using Share buttons (as a user)
- Using Share buttons (as a developer)
- Managing the shared data

Using Share Buttons (As a User)

To share data, you need one app to share the data (sometimes this process is called *vending* the data) and another app (or several apps) to receive the data and use it as the receiving app wants. Note that, just as is the case with documents and their types, the connection between sender and receiver (or vendor and receiver) is dynamic. Neither app needs to know about the other. The document type or sharing information lets each app function on its own so that you don't need to build enormous multi-purpose apps that require substantial development and maintenance costs.

© Jesse Feiler 2019
J. Feiler, *Implementing iOS and macOS Documents with the Files App*,
https://doi.org/10.1007/978-1-4842-4492-0_8

Sharing is part of Cocoa and Cocoa Touch (and it has been since the beginning of the original NeXTSTEP and Rhapsody versions of the operating systems). In order to share data, a common format needs to be available to the sender and receiver. Here is an example of the basic structure.

Creating a Sharing Example

Note   Remember that you can add apps to the simulator. Mail may not be configured for you. If you have a device you can use for testing, it's best to use it. You can test the ShareApp by downloading it as described in Chapter 1. Look for the Chapter 8 version.

The simplest example to use for sharing data is the Master-Detail project template in Xcode. It's the basis for many examples (and even apps in the App Store). It's a simple app with two views. On an iPhone, only one view at a time is shown; on larger devices, the two views share the screen. Whichever you're using, you start from an app that lets you tap + to enter the current date and time, as you can see in Figure 8-1.

Figure 8-1. *Creating a new timestamp record*

If you tap the timestamp created in the master view, you'll see the details (a better-formatted timestamp) shown in Figure 8-2.

Figure 8-2. *Detail view*

In Figure 8-3, you can see an action button added to the navigation bar at the right. (You'll learn how to implement it in this chapter). With the action button, you can share the data from the detail view.

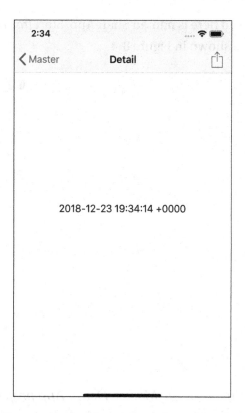

Figure 8-3. *Adding an action button to share the data*

The example used here is named ShareApp. Start from the Master-Detail App template shown in Figure 8-4.

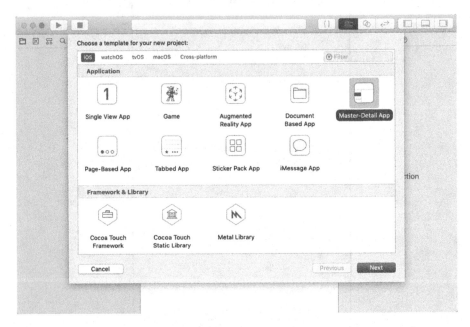

Figure 8-4. *Starting from the Master-Detail App project template*

Create your own version of the app as shown in Figure 8-5.

Figure 8-5. *Building your own project*

As you can see in Figure 8-6, you don't need to worry about any settings at this point because the defaults will work for you.

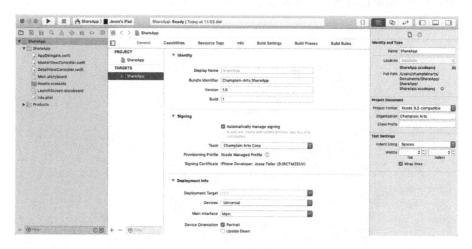

Figure 8-6. *Using the default Master-Detail App settings*

Open the storyboard. You'll see the two main views shown in Figure 8-7.

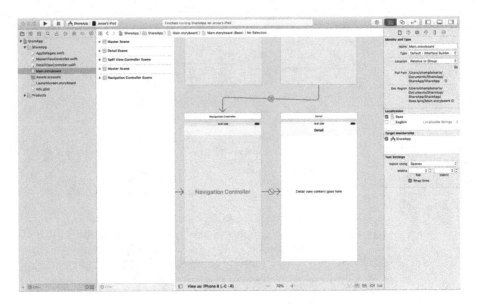

Figure 8-7. *Opening the storyboard*

Open the library at the top of the utilities pane to see the library objects, as shown in Figure 8-8.

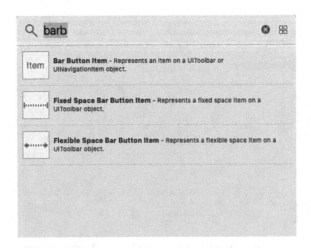

Figure 8-8. *Selecting a bar button item to add*

Drag a bar button item to the right of the top bar in the Detail scene, as shown in Figure 8-9.

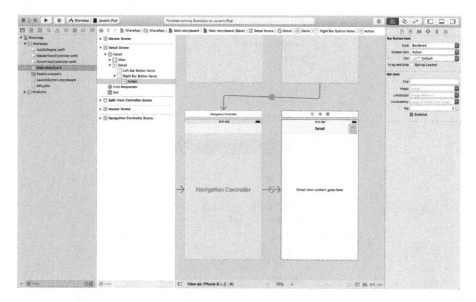

Figure 8-9. *Adding a bar button item*

From the attributes inspector, choose the Action button, as shown in Figure 8-10.

Figure 8-10. *Choosing the action button*

Implement the action button by opening the storyboard with the assistant so that you can see the storyboard and DetailViewController at the same time, as shown in Figure 8-11. Control-drag from the action button in the storyboard to the code in DetailViewController and name the outlet actionButton.

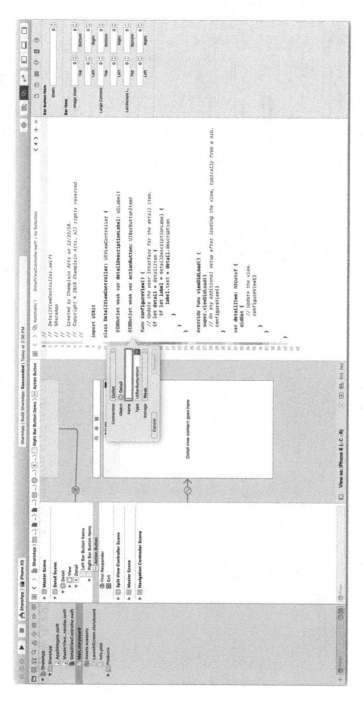

Figure 8-11. Connecting the outlet for actionButton

Add the code for the action, as shown in Figure 8-12.

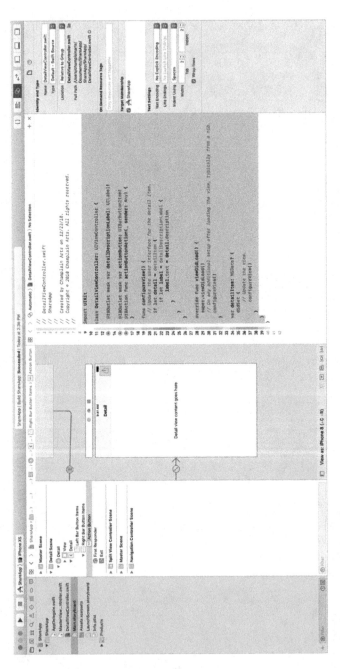

Figure 8-12. *Preparing the button and action*

Set a breakpoint in the actionButtonAction function and test that your action button now works. All that's left to do is to implement the sharing.

Sharing the Data

The objective at this point is to share the timestamp data in a format that other apps can recognize. This is done by implementing a UIActivityViewController, as you will see in this section. The activity view controller that you present will reflect the type of data that you have available to share and the possible receivers of that data. Because of this dynamic functioning, you can't be certain what you should be seeing, so the first example in this section will use a very basic type of sharing: the activity view controller will share text that is included in this section. For most users, this text will be able to be received by built-in apps such as Mail, Notes, and Messenger.

Your activity view controller will present a list of items available to share. For this example, you can do that with the code shown in Listing 8-1. Add this code to DetailViewController.

Listing 8-1. actionButtonAction

```
@IBAction func actionButtonAction(_ sender: Any) {
  let sharedItems = "Sample text"

  let activityViewController = UIActivityViewController
  (activityItems:
    [textToShare], applicationActivities: nil)

  // position the popover relative to this view
  activityViewController.popoverPresentationController?.
  sourceView = self.view

  // present the view controller
  self.present(activityViewController, animated: true,
    completion: nil)
  }
}
```

Figure 8-13. *Experimenting with an activity view controller*

In this example, you need a receiver that can handle plain text. Mail, Notes, and Messages can do so, but if you do not have them installed, your choices will be limited to Save or Copy. Otherwise, you will see an activity view controller, as shown in Figure 8-14.

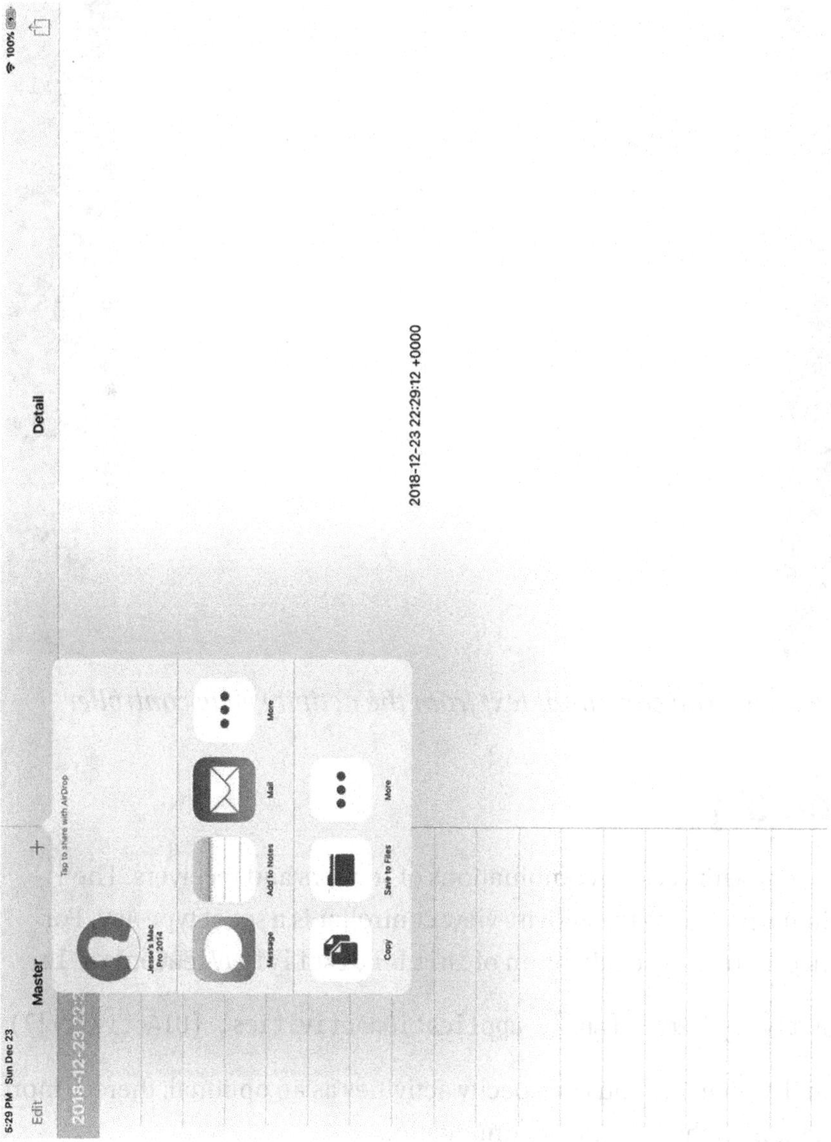

Figure 8-14. *Using the activity view controller*

If you have installed Mail, you can send the text, as shown in Figure 8-15.

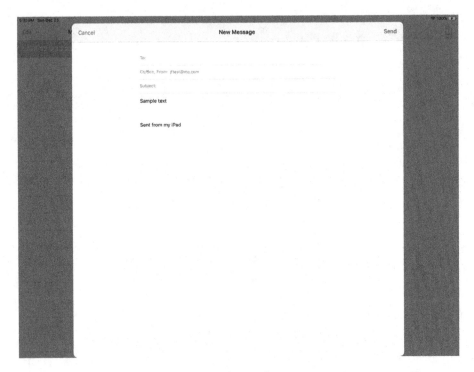

Figure 8-15. *You can email text from the activity view controller*

Summary

Experiment with various combinations of senders and receivers. The set of items passed to the activity view controller is a set of type Any. For reference, here is the declaration of init for UIActivityViewController:

```
init(activityItems: [Any], applicationActivities: [UIActivity]?)
```

You'll notice that you can specify activities as an optional; there is more information on them in the documentation.

CHAPTER 9

Using User Defaults, Settings, and Preferences

Documents are the primary way of saving data for apps. You can share the document with various apps and users so that the data is available to all users, but there are other ways to store and manage data in an app. Documents are the workhorses because you can control how much data is saved and how it is saved and shared.

Since the beginning of the iOS and macOS systems (and their predecessors) there has been another set of tools that let you store data. These tools are commonly used for user defaults, settings, and preferences. The data that they store and use is typically limited in size and scope. Even the terminology of these tools (user defaults, settings, and preferences) suggests the small size of the data involved. This remains true, but it is important to consider the fact that with the advances in technology, including data storage, user defaults, settings, and preferences, can in fact be a more central part of your app's data strategy.

© Jesse Feiler 2019
J. Feiler, *Implementing iOS and macOS Documents with the Files App*,
https://doi.org/10.1007/978-1-4842-4492-0_9

Note   Strictly speaking, a preference is the value of a setting such as the color to be used for drawing a new line where the value is blue for the `lineColor` preference. Once the value of a setting is set, it persists and is used each time the app runs until it is changed. In this case, the preference may be referred to as a *default*. In iOS, the built-in Settings app lets users control preferences and settings.

Preferences in Cocoa are stored in the Cocoa preferences system (also known as user defaults). If you want to make a strict distinction among these terms, in iOS the built-in Settings app controls these values for users. In Cocoa and Cocoa Touch, the user defaults system manages a database with the values. Some people distinguish between settings (part of the user interface) and user defaults (part of the Cocoa frameworks).

This chapter explores the possibilities you can use today for these data tools.

Looking at the Data Structures

When you are working with documents, you can control the formatting and management of the data. You can use a standard document type, which may have associated classes (images, for example), but the data for user defaults, settings, and preferences is more limited. Specifically, these objects must all be property list elements. A property list is a key-value structure where the keys are strings and the values are any of the following simple data types:

- String
- Date

- Integer number

- Float number

- Boolean

A property list (extension .plist) is designed for efficient serialization. The PropertyListSerialization class handles this for you. Property lists are used throughout Cocoa; over the years, this code has been refined and tested so that it can be relied on for many tasks.

In addition, a NSData type can be stored in a property list. If you do this, you must handle the serialization and deserialization of that data to or from an object that you want to deal with. A very common case is converting a NSData type to some binary format, which can then be interpreted as an image or other complex data structure.

Property lists can also include arrays and dictionaries. This means that you can use a property list, which itself is an array containing a dictionary that also declares another array as well as numbers and other simple objects.

The other constraint to bear in mind when considering user defaults, settings, and preferences is that the guidance from Apple is that these tools should be used only for limited purposes and relatively small amounts of data.

When thinking about storing data in this way, don't worry too much about how much data can be stored as user defaults, settings, or preferences because that's not really the limiting factor. If you use up almost all of a device's storage in this way, you will degrade performance long before you run out of space.

Property lists are stored as instances of the PropertyListSerialization class. As instances of this class, property lists are read and written in full when they are read or written. This can mean that in order to access a single Boolean value, you may need to read or write an entire property list with dozens, hundreds, or even thousands of items. You can focus your reading or writing by storing property list values in an array or dictionary, but this doesn't really help you much.

You will need to read the entire property list in order to get to the array or dictionary and only then will you be able to hone in on the value you want.

The data that is stored as defaults, preferences, and settings can be anything that you want to store (provided that it is a property list and doesn't take up too much space). There is a difference between these terms and this is a good place to start to understand them.

Exploring User Defaults, Preferences, and Settings

All of these data structures can be stored in property lists, but understanding how they are used can help you use them most efficiently. Remember that these structures are always stored in property lists, which means they are stored in key-value structures. For that reason, each user default, preference, and setting has a name (the key under which it is stored). There may be other data stored under that key—perhaps a lot of it—but each has a key.

Tip   When you are thinking about using these tools to store your own data, remember that the Settings app and user defaults system manage the data. If you want total control over the data, how it is stored, and the user interface for it, you may want to use a database or document where you control these features.

Understanding User Defaults

A user default value is a starting value (default) for some aspect of your app. For example, an app that lets you store the names of students in a class may start by identifying students as Student 1, Student 2, and so forth. A new student that a user adds might be called New Student.

In an app like this, you might want to let the users set their own defaults such as these:

- "Student" is the name of each item in the app and new items are labelled "New Student."

- You could change the default value for items to be "Item" so that you would have "Chair" and "New Chair" as the app runs.

- A slightly more complex default might let a user choose between "New" and a number to identify a new item, as in New Chair or Chair 3.

Defaults like this are often exposed to the user so that they can choose.

Tip   In a case like this, an empty string may be the default.

Exploring Settings

There is a user defaults database that stores settings like this for each app. The settings values persist from one use of the app to the next. Furthermore, users can change settings directly using the built-in tool, as shown later in this chapter.

Using Preferences

Although there is no hard-and-fast rule, many people consider preferences to be settable from outside the app, possibly even at the time the app is installed. In addition, some preferences such as the user's location or language preference are set using the operating system itself.

Preferences and Settings: A Case Study

This section uses a simple example of a setting for the name of an item in an app ("Chair" or "Student"). It shows how this can be implemented with Settings or the user defaults system rather than with a database or document.

The code for this example is downloadable as described in Chapter 1. (It is PreferencesApp.) The major steps in the process of implementing PreferencesApp are

- Start from a built-in Xcode project template (Single View App in this case).

- Add a Settings bundle to manage the settings ("Chair" or "Student" in this example).

- Build an interface to your app for the settings.

- Add an interface to show the app's settings and version. (This is useful for debugging any app. I use it automatically when I build any app.)

Creating the PreferencesApp

Because this example focuses just on settings and preferences, the Single View App project template is a good place to start (Figure 9-1).

Figure 9-1. Starting from the Single View App project template

You can use the basic settings such as naming your app. In the options shown in Figure 9-2, take a moment to look at the checkboxes at the bottom of the view. If you want to develop your own more complex preferences and other values, Core Data is a good tool to look into. It is implemented as a single user SQLite database that is built into Cocoa. If you are familiar with relational databases, it can be a good tool to use in implementing your own complex settings and preferences. When it comes to managing data in your app, you can use Settings and Core Data, as well as documents. In some cases, there are advantages to using separate data management strategies so that the app and its data are independent of one another.

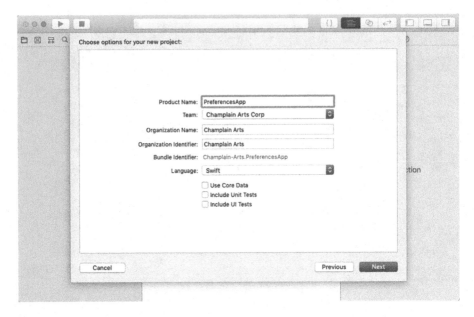

Figure 9-2. *Setting the options for PreferencesApp*

You can use the general settings shown in Figure 9-3 for PreferencesApp. It's also worth noting that PreferencesApp as implemented here doesn't require any special support in your app until you get to the integration in the "Accessing the Settings Bundle From Your Code" section later in this chapter.

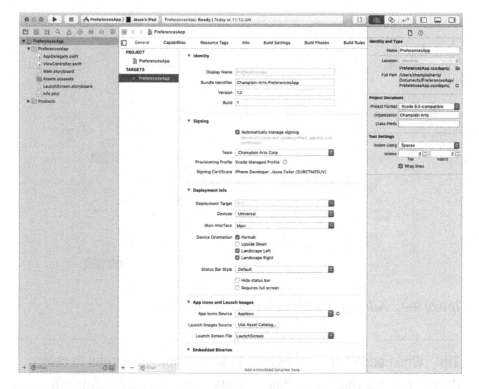

Figure 9-3. *You don't need special options to use Settings*

Adding a Settings Bundle

What you do need to do to implement Settings in an iOS app is add a
new file that contains a settings bundle. You can do this in your app using
New ➤ File, as shown in Figure 9-4.

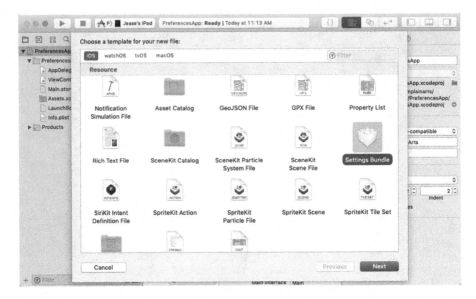

Figure 9-4. *Adding a settings bundle to your app*

Tip   When adding a settings bundle to your app, be careful to select the correct file. There are other settings bundles such as WatchKit Settings Bundle and, in the future, there are likely to be other settings bundles.

Make certain that you add the new file to the correct target in your app, as shown in Figure 9-5. (The group you place it in is important for organizing your files, but the target is absolutely essential.)

Figure 9-5. *Placing the new settings bundle in the right target*

When you have added the settings bundle, you'll see it in your project navigator, as shown in Figure 9-6.

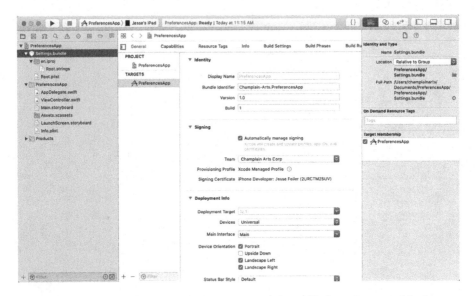

Figure 9-6. *Confirming that the settings bundle has been added to the project navigator*

Note that inside the bundle is a group (en.lproj) containing some localized strings for the root of the bundle as well as a property list of root strings. You can use these as-is. The default values are shown in Figure 9-7.

Figure 9-7. *You can use the default settings strings as-is*

With the settings bundle added to your app, you can try it out using the built-in settings. Run the app in the simulator and look for Settings, as shown in Figure 9-8.

Figure 9-8. *Using Settings in iOS*

Scroll down to find PreferencesApp, as shown in Figure 9-9.

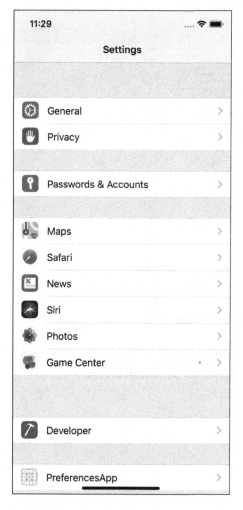

Figure 9-9. *Tapping PreferencesApp in Settings*

Open Root.plist in the settings bundle. You will see the default settings shown in Figure 9-10.

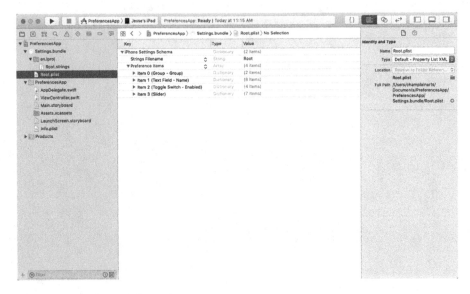

Figure 9-10. *Initial settings*

Open the Text Field item so you can see its values. Change the value of Default Value to Student, as shown in Figure 9-11.

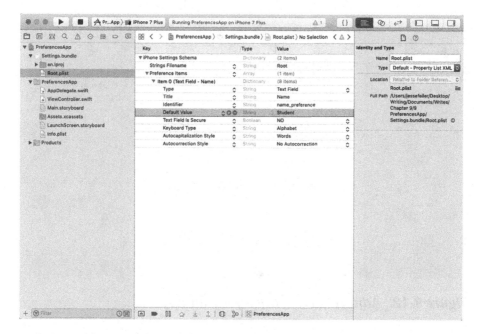

Figure 9-11. *Changing the Default Value to Student*

You can take advantage of the autocapitalization style, as you can see in Figure 9-12. This means that the words of the entered text will be capitalized. Experiment with the other Settings commands and you'll see that you have a lot of features built in that you don't have to code yourself.

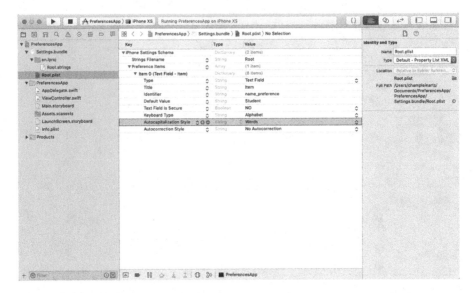

Figure 9-12. *Adjusting the settings for your app*

Finally, test Settings in the simulator, as shown in Figure 9-13. (You'll notice that some items in Settings for an app are automatically added by iOS. The Siri & Search settings are an example of this.)

Accessing the Settings Bundle from Your Code

When a user adjusts Settings, that's only the beginning. You need to be able to access the Settings values in your app. This section shows how to do so based on Settings, as shown in Figure 9-13.

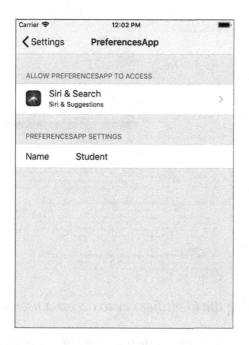

Figure 9-13. *Test settings*

Start by reminding yourself that the Settings in iOS accesses the defaults database that is built into Cocoa. That database is managed by the UserDefaults class object (not an instance; the class). UserDefaults (the class object) has a function that returns the shared defaults object with the standard property. As noted previously, each item in UserDefaults has a key, and you can access it with code such as the following:

```
return UserDefaults.standard.bool (forKey: "name_preference")
```

This key is the identifier key in the property list. As you can see in Figure 9-14, if you start to type the code to access a key, it is completed for you.

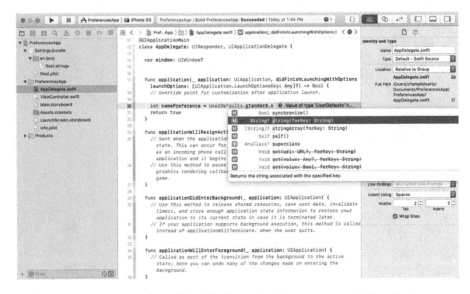

Figure 9-14. *Using the identifier key to access a user default property*

You can test this by adding code to appDelegate application(:didFi nishLaunchingWithptions:), as you can see in Figure 9-15.

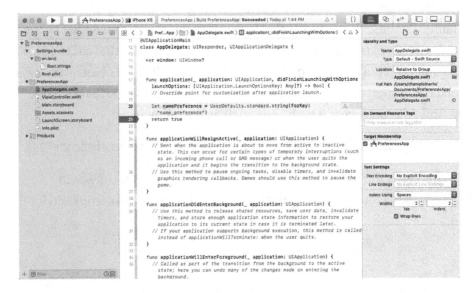

Figure 9-15. *Accessing a property in the user default Settings app*

Adding a Settings Interface

The code shown in Figure 9-15 is executed only when the app launches. You can build your own interface to show a user defaults property whenever you want it. In a view controller of the main storyboard, add a button, as shown in Figure 9-16. (If you are using the Single View App project template, as shown in this chapter, the view controller to use is called ViewController.)

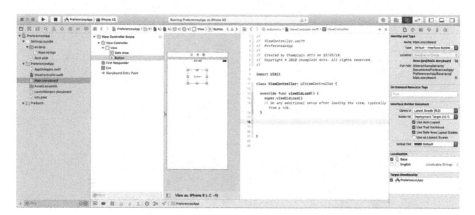

Figure 9-16. *Adding a button to the view controller*

Remember to connect the button to an action in your app, as shown in Figure 9-17.

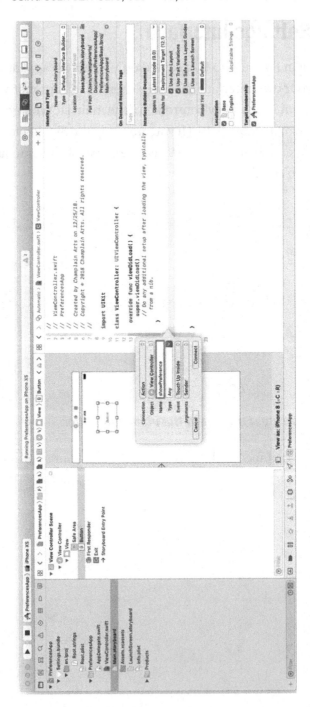

Figure 9-17. Connecting the button to an action

Add a breakpoint to the action so that you can check the value of the user default property, as shown in Figure 9-18.

Figure 9-18.   *Using a breakpoint to check the value*

Summary

This chapter showed how to use the built-in user defaults preferences and/ or Settings app to store values for your app. These values must be able to be stored in a property list and they should now be large data objects, but you can use them for many purposes other than building a large-scale data manager.

CHAPTER 10

Working with File Wrappers and Packages

This section lets you look at data storage tools other than documents. Like documents, they are all ways to persist data from your apps, and all of these tools, including documents, are supported on Cocoa and Cocoa Touch. Many of the tools (including the ones in this part of the book) have long histories in Cocoa and its predecessors. As noted, documents have evolved over time and have changed in many ways. The tools in this section have certainly changed over time, but the basic structures have remained remarkably stable so they are used in many legacy apps as well as in ones being developed today.

All of the tools in this chapter let you combine files into multi-file structures that can be manipulated either as single structures or as their component parts.

Using Packages

From early days of Macintosh, multi-file packages have been used to manage files. In the first Macintosh file system, files had two sections called *forks*. Almost all files had a *data fork*, and many files also had a *resource fork*. The user-visible file was basically the data fork, and the resource fork contained elements that the data fork used. These elements were typically alerts, icons, and other identifiable or visible elements. Each type of element in a resource fork had a name, typically a four-character code such as ALRT (for alert), DLOG (for dialog), or ICON. The idea of using identifiable and structured elements in a container remains a critical part of Cocoa.

The disadvantage of the resource fork was that when you copied a file to another platform the resource fork typically disappeared; it was the data fork that contained the data so it wasn't a disaster in most cases. Today, Cocoa (and Cocoa Touch) use a more sophisticated way of wrapping data into what appears to be a single file. They are referred to as *packages*.

Note   Swift packages are manifests that are used to assemble code and manage dependencies. A common tool is CocoaPods (CocoaPods.org).

You can still see packages throughout Cocoa and particularly in the developer tools. When you create a project in Xcode, you usually create a folder that contains two items, shown in Figure 10-1.

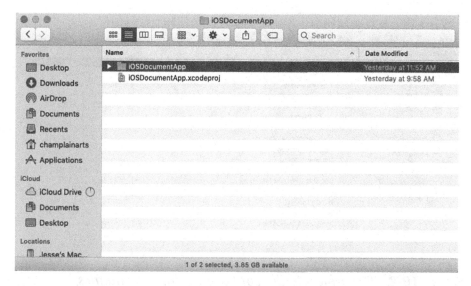

Figure 10-1. *An Xcode project consists of a file and a folder*

In the example shown in Figure 10-1, the name of the project is iOSDocumentApp. The project itself is in an xcodeproj file, which contains references to the iOSDocumentApp folder. The open folder is shown in Figure 10-2. Note that inside the folder are individual files as well as subfolders with more files and folders.

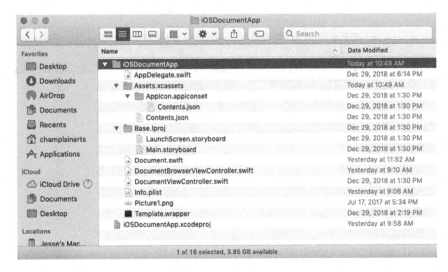

Figure 10-2. *The project folder contains subfolders and files*

If you hold down Control while clicking a file or folder in the Finder, you will see the contents of that file or folder as a package. This is shown in Figure 10-3.

Figure 10-3. *Use the Control key to look inside a file package*

Note that not all files or folders are packages, so the Control key cannot open them. However, it is important to note that your Xcode project is a package of files. If you move the folder away from the xcodeproj file that refers to it, you will break the project package.

Inside a file package, the contents are often structured with a Contents folder that contains subfolders, as you can see in Figure 10-4. Most apps have a Contents folder.

Figure 10-4. *Files and folders can be structured within the package*

Considering Bundles

If you look at build phases in an Xcode app, you'll see a step that moves files into an app bundle, as shown in Figure 10-5.

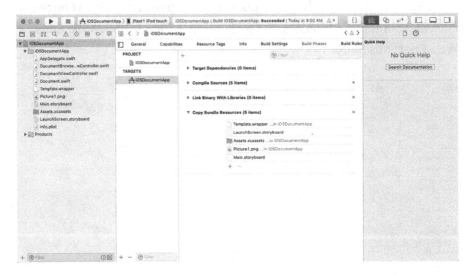

Figure 10-5. *Apps contain bundles*

When you add files to an app in the project navigator, they are usually automatically added to the Build Phases step so that they are found in the app bundle, and that's where you can retrieve them from in your code. By default, your app has a main bundle (`bundle.main`) with known contents. You can find the API at `developer.apple.com` by looking for *bundle*.

Using File Wrappers

File wrappers are somewhat similar to packages in that they may contain files and folders inside a single object. A file wrapper typically has at least one file, but it can be empty. File wrappers are most frequently used as the container for files and folders in a document that itself is a file wrapper. Figure 10-6 shows a file wrapper document.

Figure 10-6. *Declaring a file wrapper document*

Note that you need to set the `LSTypeIsPackage` property to YES so that the document appears to the user as a single object. The file type should conform to `com.apple.package`.

You can download `WrapperPlaygroundDemo` as described in Chapter 1 to see how to put a file wrapper document together. The process is described in the following section. The code is shown in Listing 10-1.

The process is simple:

- Assemble the files that will be wrapped.

- Convert each file to the Data type (formerly NSData). There are utility methods in Swift to do this easily.

- Wrap each file in a wrapper.

- Create a root wrapper in the document.

- Add each wrapped file to the root wrapper.

You can do these steps in any order, and there are functions that let you add and remove them dynamically. One common use of file wrappers is to wrap together several related files such as media and text. If they are wrapped in a file wrapper, you use the `contents(forType:)` and `load(fromContents:ofType:)` methods as you would for a document that consists of any data type such as an archive or a single image or text.

The files in the root file wrapper are not in any given order. Most important for reasons of efficiency is the fact that each file wrapper is loaded separately so if you have a lot of files in a single object, you can load them on an as-needed basis (Swift and Cocoa take care of this for you).

Listing 10-1 shows the code to assemble a file wrapper from files named `testString` and `testImage`; they are each wrapped in an individual wrapper (the names are `stringDataWrapper` and `imageDataWrapper`). In addition, there is a `rootDirectoryWrapper`. As noted in the code at the end of Listing 10-1, you can read or write the wrapped files using `contents(forType:)` or `load(fromContents:ofType:)`.

Listing 10-1. Assembling a File Wrapper Document in a Playground

```
import UIKit
import PlaygroundSupport

let testString = "Now is the time"
let testImage = UIImage(named:"mantegna.jpg")

// convert to Data
let imageData = testImage!.pngData()
let stringData = testString.data (using: .utf8)

// build directory wrapper
let rootDirectoryWrapper = FileWrapper(directoryWithFile
Wrappers: [:])
```

```
// wrap string
let stringDataWrapper = FileWrapper(regularFileWithContents:
stringData!)
stringDataWrapper.preferredFilename = "StringWrapper"
rootDirectoryWrapper.addFileWrapper(stringDataWrapper)

// wrap image
let imageDataWrapper = FileWrapper(regularFileWithContents:
imageData!)
imageDataWrapper.preferredFilename = "ImageWrapper"
rootDirectoryWrapper.addFileWrapper(imageDataWrapper)

print ("wrapper", rootDirectoryWrapper)
print (rootDirectoryWrapper.fileWrappers)
for eachWrapper in rootDirectoryWrapper.fileWrappers! {
  print (eachWrapper)
}

// for writing: return rootDirectoryWrapper if you are using in
contents(forType:)
// for reading: load(fromContents:ofType:)
```

Summary

This chapter showed how to wrap files together in bundles or file wrappers. There are efficiencies to using file wrappers since only necessary file wrappers are updated as the root file wrapper is managed. The overall idea of having a way to handle files separately or together depending on what you want to do with them is the key take-away from wrappers and bundles.

CHAPTER 11

Using File Archives

In Chapter 7, you learned the basics of reading and writing document data. One common way of doing this is to convert your own data from whatever its structure and format is to an NSData object (now a Data object), which can be read or written with a simple statement. The only catch to this is that you need to do the conversion from your data type to Data. One of the simplest and most used techniques is to use the built-in archiving technology in Cocoa.

Note Archiving is gradually being replaced by Codable, but the transition is ongoing. Older code generally uses archiving as described in this chapter. You can find Apple's documentation of both at https://developer.apple.com/documentation/ foundation/archives_and_serialization. Also, the latest version of Swift NSData has become Data.

This chapter provides an overview of archiving. The example is a common use of archiving in which you take some data, archive it to Data, and then unarchive it to (hopefully) the original value. This is such a useful process that many developers leave code of this nature commented out in apps so that it can be monitored during debugging by simply enabling the code.

© Jesse Feiler 2019
J. Feiler, *Implementing iOS and macOS Documents with the Files App*,
https://doi.org/10.1007/978-1-4842-4492-0_11

Using Swift Unified Logging

The archiving and debugging code in this chapter is implemented using the Swift Unified Logging System available in iOS 10, macOS 10, tvOS 10, and watch OS 3 (as well as later versions of these products). Unified logging is a modern and efficient tool that replaces previous tools such as Apple System Logger (ASL). It is possible to move to unified logging as you are working on new sections of code, so developers are gradually doing so. This section provides a quick overview of unified logging as an introduction. For more information, go to the Apple documentation at `https://developer.apple.com/documentation/os/logging`.

The heart of unified logging is a data type that contains information about the logged information. (This replaces previous iterations of logging in which parameters were passed to a function.) If you use unified logging, you can construct your own structure for your logging. The version of 11 ShareApp (downloadable as described in Chapter 1) uses a common version. It is a `struct` defined with the code shown in Listing 11-1.

Listing 11-1. Commonly used Log Structure

```
// Use new Swift unified logging system
import os.log
struct Log {
  static var general = OSLog(subsystem: "com.myapp.my_target",
                             category: "info")
}
```

This code is shown in Figure 11-1.

Figure 11-1. *Importing os.log and defining the struct*

In the example, this code is placed at the top of `AppDelegate.swift`. You use the code where needed in your app, as you will see in this section. The invocation in a minimal version is like this code:

```
os_log("Row selected-%@",
        indexPath.debugDescription)
```

Beyond the bare minimum here, refer to the documentation cited previously for other information you can log. As a result of this code, here is what will be shown in the console:

```
2018-12-26 14:51:09.777111-0500 ShareApp[6228:697878]
  Row selected-[0, 0]
```

This causes an invocation of OSLog. Beyond the parameters shown here, you can add additional parameters such as the standard formatting for a print statement, like

```
("Row selected-%@",
```

and a string that is generated dynamically and formatted according to that command.

You will see this in action later in this chapter.

Using Log and a Breakpoint to Archive Data

If you use archiving to encode and decode data for the `contents(forType:)` and `load (fromContents:, ofType:)` functions, it is useful to test that code with a breakpoint. Once things are tested, you can use archiving in the actual functions.

Returning to ShareApp, you can intercept a tap in a timestamp generated in the master view controller and attempt to encode it. Figure 11-2 reminds you of the master view controller in which you can add new timestamp items with the +.

Figure 11-2. *Adding new timestamps with +*

As noted, it is common to work with the master detail view controller as a starting point for many apps. In the master detail model, you can add functionality at either the master or detail level. Users are accustomed to this interface, so it makes sense not to add an unfamiliar variation. If you add a Share button to the master view controller, as shown in Figure 11-3, users will expect to share the contents of the master view controller, which is all of the data.

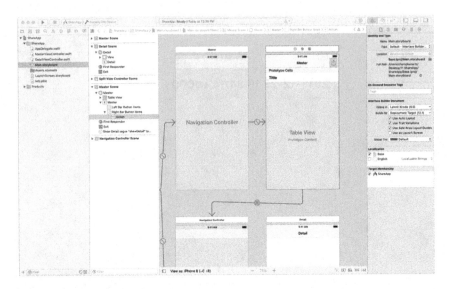

Figure 11-3. *Sharing the master view controller data*

But what do you do if you want to share a single item? There are two approaches you can take. One is to put a Share button on a detail view controller, as you can see in Figure 11-4.

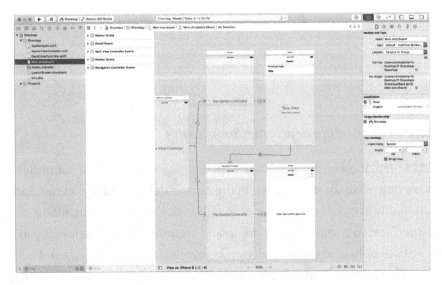

Figure 11-4. *Sharing from a detail view controller*

When using the master detail model, you have to remember that it is the master item that manages the detail items. This means that the control for selecting one of the detail items belongs on the master view controller because it is the master that will manage the selection of the detail item.

If it is the master that will be handling selection, where do you put the Share button so that it is not confused with a Share button that selects everything? The most common solution is to simply use a tap or click in a detail row of the master view controller to manage selection. This is an efficient way to proceed (and it takes advantage of a useful function).

The function that lets you select a single detail item from the master view controller is the UITableViewDelegate function named tableView(_:didSelectRowAt:).

Figure 11-5 shows how to override that function with a log message. (The log message adds log and type variables to the minimal code in Listing 11-1).

The code shows a console message identifying which detail item has been selected, as you can see in Figure 11-5.

Figure 11-5. *Log selection of a detail item*

Selecting the Item to Archive

To get started with the archive, create a breakpoint so that you can access the selected item. You do so in the tableView(_:didSelectRowAt:) function, as shown in Listing 11-2.

Listing 11-2. Showing the Selected Object

```
override func tableView(_ tableView: UITableView,
  didSelectRowAt indexPath: IndexPath) {
    //let rowDebugDescription = indexPath.debugDescription

    os_log("Row selected-%@",
          type: .info,
          indexPath.debugDescription)

  // set a breakpoint here
    let object = objects[indexPath.row] as! NSDate
  }
```

Figure 11-6 shows the simulator and the data in this test.

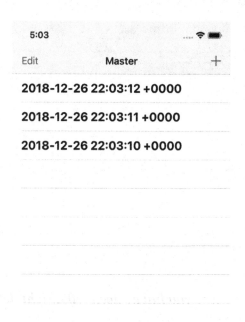

Figure 11-6. *Data in the simulator for testing*

When the item is selected in the simulator, the breakpoint is triggered, as you can see in Figure 11-7.

Figure 11-7. *Make sure you have selected the right detail object*

This experiment requires that you correctly capture the detail item so make certain that you have done so. (In this sample, make sure you have created at least two detail items so that you can use the timestamps to differentiate between them.)

Creating the Object to Archive

ShareApp creates new objects in the master view controller that it then can display. These objects are NSDate objects with the current timestamp. When you start thinking about archiving objects, you can continue with these NSDate objects, but in real life, you will probably use custom objects that you archive. For that reason, a new object (ShareableObject) can be created here to use in your archiving tests. SharableObject will actually wrap an NSDate object, so the changes to the app are relatively few. (Not only are they relatively few, but if you are using this app as the basis of other projects, you'll repeat these modifications for each one.)

The first step is to create the new `SharableObject` class which wraps an `NSDate` object, which can be called `sharableDate`. As always, create the new class in Xcode using File ➤ New ➤ File to create a new Cocoa Touch Class for iOS, as you can see in Figure 11-8.

Figure 11-8. *Creating a new class for ShareableObject*

Name the new class as `SharableObject`, as shown in Figure 11-9.

Figure 11-9. *This will need to be a subclass of `NSObject`*

As always, when you add a new class to a project, make certain it is in the right target, as shown in Figure 11-10.

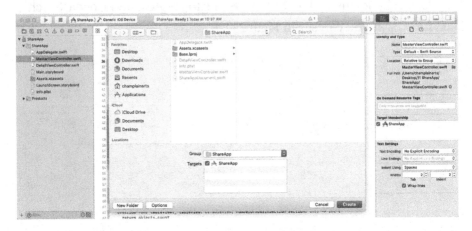

Figure 11-10. *Adding the new class to the target*

Add the `sharableDate` property to `SharableObject`, as shown in Figure 11-11.

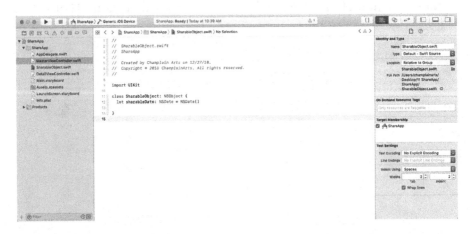

Figure 11-11. *Creating the class*

Make a few changes so that instead of creating a new NSDate when you add an object to the app, you create a new ShareableObject. Similarly, you update the interface to show the date that is inside ShareableObject. These are common changes that are quickly shown in the following section.

In MasterViewController, insertNewObject will have to insert a new ShareableObject. Listing 11-3 shows the updated function.

Listing 11-3. Inserting a new ShareableObject

```
@objc
  func insertNewObject(_ sender: Any) {
    //objects.insert(NSDate(), at: 0)
    objects.insert(SharableObject(), at: 0)
    let indexPath = IndexPath(row: 0, section: 0)
    tableView.insertRows(at: [indexPath], with: .automatic)
  }
```

Change MasterViewController as shown in Listing 11-4 to show the description of the sharableDate object.

Listing 11-4. Showing the Date

```
  override func tableView(_ tableView: UITableView,
    cellForRowAt indexPath: IndexPath) -> UITableViewCell {
    let cell = tableView.dequeueReusableCell(withIdentifier:
    "Cell", for: indexPath)

    let object = objects[indexPath.row] as! SharableObject
    cell.textLabel!.text = object.sharableDate.description
    return cell
  }
```

Try running the app. It should look like the original version, but if you set a breakpoint, you should be able to see that you're showing the description of sharableDate.

Doing the Archive

Now that you have the item to archive, you can archive it and proceed to unarchive it to test the process. To use the archiving tools, you need to implement the NSCoder protocol in the class to be archived (or unarchived). This structure means that each object encodes or decodes itself. You see this over and over in Cocoa apps: each object does its own work as much as possible. This means that when you make changes to the app, you minimize where the changes are made. If you want to go through the changes in the previous section, you'll see that changing NSDate to Sha rableObject/shareableDate doesn't require much rewriting of code.

Making the Class Conform to NSCoding

When you create the SharableObject class, you make it a subclass of NSObject, and you also make it conform to NSCoding, which does the archiving. By simply adding NSCoding to the class, you will generate some errors. Xcode will ask if you want it to automatically add stubs for the missing functions, as you can see in Figure 11-12.

This will get you on your way to completing the app.

Figure 11-12. *Xcode can add stubs for NSCoding functions*

When you tap Fix, the stubs will be added, as you can see in Figure 11-13.

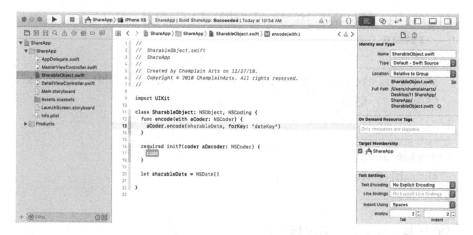

Figure 11-13. *Letting Xcode add stubs for NSCoding*

Complete the stubs with the code shown in Listing 11-5.

Listing 11-5. Complete sharableObject

```
import UIKit
import os.log

class SharableObject: NSObject, NSCoding {
  var sharableDate: NSDate=NSDate()

   func encode(with aCoder: NSCoder) {
    aCoder.encode(self.sharableDate, forKey: "dateKey")
  }

  required init?(coder aDecoder: NSCoder) {
    guard (aDecoder.decodeObject(forKey: "dateKey") as? NSDate)
    != nil else
    {
      os_log ("Unable to decode sharableDate")
      return
    }
    sharableDate = aDecoder.decodeObject(forKey: "dateKey") as?
    NSDate ?? NSDate()
  }

  override init() {
    sharableDate = NSDate()
  }

  init(dateToInit: NSDate) {
    sharableDate = dateToInit
  }
}
```

The functions that you add all take an NSCoder called aCoder as a
parameter. It is passed in so you don't declare it. The encode(with:)
function lets you encode data for the archive. The typical use of this

function is to encode one variable in the class and to give it a key name. By doing this, you can access each variable in the archive by a key name and you don't have to worry about the order of the data in the file. In Listing 11-5, the first encode function encodes the sharableDate property and assigns the key dateKey to it.

The companion function, init(coder:), takes a Decoder object and reverses the process.

Implementing the Example

The stub code needs to be entered for most archiving processes. For the example, you can move beyond tableView(:didSelectRowAt:) so that you can archive and dearchive data for testing. This section is only for testing. The example code is shown in Listing 11-6.

Listing 11-6. Implement Debugginng Code in the Example

```
override func tableView(_ tableView: UITableView,
didSelectRowAt indexPath: IndexPath) {

  os_log("Row selected-%@",
          indexPath.debugDescription)

  let object = objects[indexPath.row] as! SharableObject

  var savedData: Data?

  do {
    let data = try NSKeyedArchiver.archivedData(withRootObject:
    object,
      requiringSecureCoding: false)
    try data.write(to: MasterViewController.ArchiveURL)
    savedData = data as Data // keep it around for testing later
```

```
  } catch {
    os_log ("Couldn't write file")
  }

do {
let debuggedUnArchive = try
  NSKeyedUnarchiver.unarchiveTopLevelObjectWithData(savedData!
  as Data)
    if let test = debuggedUnArchive as? SharableObject {
      print ("\(test.sharableDate)")
    }
  } catch {
    os_log ("Couldn't read file")
  }
```

The heart of the archiving code is this line:

```
let data = try NSKeyedArchiver.archivedData(withRootObject:
object,
```

It invokes the stubs you created to archive the class into a Data object called data. This line of code takes the Data object and unarchives it into a variable called test in Listing 11-6.

The process of unarchiving and archiving data that is shown here uses a temporary file that you can create. It is shown at the top of MasterViewController with these lines:

```
static let DocumentsDirectory = FileManager().urls(
  for:.documentDirectory,
  in: .userDomainMask).first!
static let ArchiveURL = DocumentsDirectory.appendingPathComponent
("sharableObjectURL")
```

Set breakpoints and experiment with the code to see how it works. This is the common archiving code that you will frequently use.

Moving Archiving into Documents

Instead of moving data to and from a file, you will frequently want to move it into and out of a document that can be shared with other users. Simply change the UIDocument functions to do archiving and dearchiving. This means that contents(forType:) will use NSKeyedArchiver. archivedData(withRootObject: requiringSecureCoding:) to archive the data to an Data object and load(fromContents:, ofType) will use NSKeyedUnarchiver.unarchiveTopLevelObjectWithData() to reverse the archive operation.

For reference, Listing 11-7 shows the stubs of the UIDocument functions that you will use in this way.

Listing 11-7. Please Add Caption

```
import UIKit

class Document: UIDocument {

  override func contents(forType typeName: String) throws -> Any {
    // Encode your document with an instance of Data or
    NSFileWrapper
    return Data()
  }

  override func load(fromContents contents: Any, ofType
  typeName: String?)
    throws {
      // Load your document from contents: ofType:)
    }
}
```

Summary

In this chapter, you saw how to archive and unarchive data to a file. You can use the same process to work with a document. Try the process as described in this chapter and set breakpoints as you test it. It may take a little while to try it out, but once you have mastered archiving and unarchiving, you are ready to move on to more complex documents.

Index

© Jesse Feiler 2019
J. Feiler, *Implementing iOS and macOS Documents with the Files App*,
https://doi.org/10.1007/978-1-4842-4492-0

V, W

X, Y, Z

Printed in the United States
By Bookmasters